PRAISE FOR
STEPPING ON THE BLENDER

Katherine Snow Smith is a five-star storyteller, and the thing is, you don't just want to read her book, you want to be friends with her. Readable, relatable, fun, funny, poignant and occasionally piercing, *Stepping on the Blender* is like sitting with a buddy who tells the best tales because she knows exactly when to cut to the chase and always leaves you wanting more. I did not want to put this book down, and neither will you.

—**Frances Schultz**, author, *The Bee Cottage Story*

Katherine Snow Smith's punch to our emotions proves she truly has wordsmithing in her DNA, as she follows in the footsteps of her father, A.C. Snow, editor and long-time Raleigh columnist who engaged North Carolina readers for 70 years. Katherine highlights her—and our—everyday dilemmas, dramas and delights with humor and honesty.

—**Jan Yopp**, co-author, *Reaching Audiences: A Guide to Media Writing*

By writing openly and honestly about her exciting firsts, interim changes, unexpected joys, and sad but inevitable goodbyes, Katherine Snow Smith's prose invites us to reflect on and be grateful for our own stories—what we should remember and try never to forget—because time marches on, even when you step on a blender.

—**Landis Wade**, Charlotte Readers Podcast founder and award-winning writer

Stepping on the Blender

Stepping on the Blender

on the

Blender

&

Other Times Life Gets Messy

Katherine Snow Smith

LYSTRA BOOKS
Literary Services

ISBN 979-8-9877247-0-5 paperback
ISBN 919-8- 9877247-1-2 ebook
Library of Congress Control Number 2023918181

Illustrations: Alli Arnold
Cover photo and author's portrait: Zack Wittman
Illustration of Book Pocketbooks logo: Lee Burgess
Book design: Kelly Prelipp Lojk

LYSTRA BOOKS
&t Literary Services

Published by
Lystra Books & Literary Services, LLC
391 Lystra Estates Drive, Chapel Hill, NC 27517
lystrabooks@gmail.com

To Olivia, Charlotte and Wade

— Contents —

— Foreword —

The car was almost packed, and I was only 20 minutes behind my target departure time for the drive from Florida to North Carolina. My house was spotless and ready for renters for four months while I was away. I glanced around my kitchen one last time and decided to put the frosted glasses with merry-go-round animals in the cabinet above the refrigerator.

The tall, slim glasses with the blue-and-white tiger, yellow giraffe, orange elephant and other cheerful mammals were a wedding present to my parents in 1958. When I was growing up, they were only used for milkshakes made in the blender for my sister and me. I had reserved them for the same purpose with my three children. Now the vintage glasses sat on a shelf over the sink reminding me of three generations of my family. I didn't want to risk the renters breaking one.

I climbed onto a kitchen chair to move each glass to safer ground. When I leaned down for the last one, my elbow hit my Ninja blender, knocking it from the counter to the floor. I gasped, but the plastic pitcher bounced without breaking, and the blade rattled onto the tile.

Katherine Snow Smith

"That was a close one. I am so lucky," I said aloud. I secured my glass menagerie into the cabinet and was ready to hit the road.

I stepped down without looking, and my left foot landed on the blender blade, which dug a good two inches into my bare heel. I fell to the floor and screamed as I pulled the blade out of my foot. A geyser of blood erupted.

"No. No. No. Noooooooo. Please. No," I wailed and started crying. "Not now. I was so close. Damn it."

My phone and towels were across the house in my bedroom, so I crawled from the kitchen, through the living room and grabbed one of the fresh teal towels I'd just hung up for the renters. It turned scarlet in the minute it took to call my friend Deann, my usual medical advisor since she was an obstetrics nurse more than 25 years ago.

No answer.

I called another friend, Burchie, who has no medical training but lived nearby.

"Burchie! I stepped on the blender and there's blood everywhere and I've got to drive to North Carolina," I sobbed. "I give up. I give up. I can't do this anymore."

"Holy moly, Katherine. I'm getting in my car right now. I'm on my way to your house," she said. "Should you call 9-1-1?"

"I'm not dying. It just won't stop bleeding."

"I'll take you to the emergency room. They can stitch it right up."

"I don't have time for the emergency room. I have a book signing in St. Marys, Georgia, tonight. I need to leave in 20 minutes to make it there in time."

"You need to cancel that. I'm walking in your door right now," she said as I heard it open.

"Katherine! Look at all this blood." Burchie followed the scarlet trail to my bedroom. "We are going to the hospital right now."

"I can't. Even if I don't do the book signing, I have to be in Chapel Hill the day after tomorrow to start teaching. If I don't leave today, I won't make it there in time."

Just then, Deann returned my call, and I explained the situation to her while Burchie took over holding another towel to my foot. Deann called back on FaceTime to survey the damage.

"Burchie, can you hold the phone right over the cut?" our medical adviser asked.

"I keep wiping off the blood to see the cut, but it just comes back," Burchie said.

"Okay. Just keep putting pressure on it," Deann advised.

At this point I was lying on my back on my bedroom floor with my foot propped up against a chair while Burchie held the third or fourth towel against it.

"So is there blood everywhere?" Deann asked.

"Did you see *The Staircase*?" Burchie asked. "It's kind of like that."

Finally, the bleeding stopped for a whole five minutes, and Deann got a good look at the gash in my heel. It was a straight slit with no jagged edges or tissue and tendons oozing out. Though I couldn't put any weight on my foot, I could move it in all directions.

"I think you may be okay without stitches," Deann said. "Try to get some of those liquid stitches they sell at CVS or Walgreens. And it's good it's your left foot. Maybe you can keep it elevated while you drive."

Burchie loaded the last suitcases and my printer in the car.

xiv

"You're going to be okay, Katherine. You're going to be more than okay," she said, hugging me goodbye. "But please know I'm never having another margarita or smoothie at your house."

I drove up Interstate 95 with my left foot wrapped in a blue bandage, propped up on the dashboard between the steering wheel and window, and headed into the next phase of my life.

Molly, another St. Petersburg friend, called me in the car. She'd heard the news from Deann. She admonished me for not having stopped yet to get the liquid stitches and I whined that I didn't have time. A few minutes later she called back to give me the address of a Walgreens in St. Marys. She had already confirmed they sold liquid stitches.

"It will take you five minutes to stop there. And please tell me you are wearing a shoe or a sock to keep it from getting infected," she said because she knew me well enough to know that of course I was barefooted.

I made it to the St. Marys Walgreens and then to my little inn on the river with just enough time to ooze the "stitches" onto my foot, cover it in a white sock and put on tennis shoes with my linen shift. I hobbled into the book signing at a local gift and furniture store called Cottle & Gunn. I read an essay from my first book about the time I fell off my high heels while getting my photo taken with President Barack Obama at a White House media party.

"Are you still limping from that?" an observant woman in the audience asked.

"Oh no. This is from stepping on the blender this morning," I replied, then laughed at myself. If I wasn't falling on a president, I was stepping on a blender.

As I continued up I-95 the next day, I really tried to

figure out why these mishaps happen to me way too frequently. Am I accident prone or just unlucky? Careless or simply an idiot? Things do seem to go wrong. A lot. And not just injuries. I thought of the time the Uber taking me to the airport broke down on the Howard Frankland Bridge between St. Petersburg and Tampa. I had to get to Raleigh that day because of something or other with my parents, so I got out and walked along the edge of the bridge for a couple miles or so, pulling my carry-on behind me. My friend Biz happened to call and made me take a selfie, which showed my suitcase, four lanes of traffic behind me, and Tampa Bay's white caps lapping at the side of the bridge.

Two women who thought I had chosen to get out of a car because I was trying to get away from someone stopped and offered me a ride. I made it to my gate with 45 minutes to spare.

"Katherine, these things only happen to you," people said when I recounted the incident.

But it's not just me.

We all step on the blender at various points in life. Things go awry for everyone. From flat tires to cancerous tumors, broken Ubers to broken marriages, losing a wallet to losing a child, sister, spouse, friend, or parent. Some wounds are fine with a few liquid stitches, and some never heal.

I guess people like me, who cram too many things into a day or change course at the last minute are more ripe for mishap. I don't always calculate the risks, and when I do, I don't always pay heed to them. This increases my margin of error. I do bring some of this on myself. But a lot of the tough times in life just happen randomly with no chance of preventing them. Plenty of times in my life, I've passed right on by the Ninja blades and been very fortunate.

We all step on the blender and keep moving through life with various-sized scars. Some scars trace pain and resilience or risk and triumph while others become laugh lines. They shape us, prepare us for subsequent wounds and make us better at holding the towel for someone else's bleeding foot.

*In the long run, a people is known,
not by its statements or its statistics,
but by the stories it tells.*

–Flannery O'Connor

— 1 —

Home Again

I couldn't escape the irony displayed on my bathroom counter as I dried my hair before going to see the Connells, a favorite college band from the '80s.

A 32-ounce bottle of MiraLAX touting its "easy to pour lid" sat next to a small bottle of L'Oréal's Magic Root Cover Up. A blood pressure cuff dangled into the sink.

Yep. A few things had changed since I last saw the Connells back in college.

But here I was, living in Chapel Hill again, three decades after graduating from the University of North Carolina.

A couple weeks into my temporary move to Chapel Hill to be closer to my parents in Raleigh, I was getting used to how much things had changed since I was a student. The standard apparel for college girls basically is an exercise bra and leggings—with an unzipped hoodie on cold days. The legendary Rathskeller on Franklin Street, a beloved restaurant and bar since 1948 known as The Rat is now a craft brewery. Ye Olde Waffle Shoppe sits empty, surrounded by CBD stores. The Target that replaced a cluster of local shops sells mostly White Claws and the aforementioned exercise bras and leggings. And the Happy Store, a little gas station where we bought beer back in the day, is now a four-story restaurant and bar.

The fall of 2021 was the first time I'd lived in my native North Carolina since getting married and moving to St. Petersburg, Florida, in 1993. Thirty years later I was divorced, my last child had just left for college, and my work was remote so there was nothing keeping me in Florida. I rented out my St. Petersburg bungalow, found an Airbnb in Chapel Hill and was able to visit my aging parents every few days.

"I don't know, Kat," my longtime friend Marjorie said, pausing to take a swig of Sonoma-Cutrer, when she visited me in Chapel Hill. "This may not be the best thing for your psyche."

She was right.

It took me a while to figure out it wasn't the changing landscape or different ways of yet another generation of college kids that made living in Chapel Hill harder than I expected.

It was how much I have changed.

I don't mean those pesky little gray hairs around my temples, the high blood pressure or the slightly irregular digestive tract after a small bout with colon cancer. I'm talking about how much my life has changed.

Last time I was in Chapel Hill, a blank canvas and endless years lay ahead of me. I was going to be a hard-nosed reporter going into dangerous situations to expose corruption and write gripping narratives of struggles and triumphs. I envisioned a *New York Times* or *Chicago Tribune* byline.

I also pictured meeting the man of my dreams, raising a family and growing old together.

I never made it to New York or Chicago, but did love working at several papers throughout the south, including a 20-year stint at the *Tampa Bay Times*. I married someone I met when we worked at competing newspapers in South Carolina. We raised three children and had many good times but divorced after 24 years. Obviously, there were some tough times too.

I've enjoyed plenty and accomplished a lot since graduating college. But frankly, the juxtaposition from the last time I lived in Chapel Hill to now was depressing. My whole life is no longer before me; I'm starting over with less time on the clock and more baggage.

I was also bothered by what hadn't changed. On the one hand—the hand that still has a wedding-ring tan line years after we signed the papers—I'm a successful journalist, author, mother and dedicated daughter. On the other hand—on which I wear a ring made from one of my father's 1950 Old Well cufflinks—I feel untethered, ungrounded and very much on my own. I've aged but haven't grown up as much as I feel I should have.

I still rush out the door eating a heaping spoon of peanut butter for breakfast several days a week. I put makeup on at stop lights because I'm always getting ready at the last minute. Even if I had an extra 10 minutes to look in a bathroom mirror with perfect lighting, there's really no point because I have no idea how to blend or contour.

My fingernails look like I get manicures from Edward Scissorhands.

I can be too outspoken. I wear my heart on my sleeve.

Since I turned 16, I get at least two flat tires a year because I hit curbs. I manage to be a bad driver while also being an overly cautious one, rarely going five miles over the speed limit. I recently saw a bumper sticker for sale at a gas station reading: "If I just passed you on the right, you're an idiot." I am that idiot.

While most people my age are streaming documentaries about elephant whisperers or binging on the hottest HBO Max release, I'm watching reruns of The *Mary Tyler Moore Show*, *Will and Grace* and *Everybody Loves Raymond*. (If you get nothing else from this book, please take this away from it. *Everybody Loves Raymond* is as smart and hilarious as anything you can stream. I never watched it until Paul Rudd gave the Emmy-pa-looza TV show a shoutout in *The 40-Year-Old Virgin* in 2005.)

I write checks out of numerical order from whatever tattered checkbook I can find in a kitchen drawer or under the passenger seat of my car—next to my long-lost mascara.

I still write checks.

Now, to be fair to my situation in North Carolina, the scenario is about the same when I'm living in St. Petersburg. I think my weaknesses and challenges hit me harder in Chapel Hill because I thought living in my beloved home state again after 26 years in Florida would be like easing into a pair of well-worn slippers. But here I was back where I started with no idea what my future held, what I wanted it to hold or what I could do to get there even if I did know.

Cue one of UNC's most notable alum's famous words: You can't go home again. This is the title of Thomas Wolfe's book that was published posthumously in 1940. That was

10 years after he won the Nobel Prize for Literature. His first critically acclaimed biographical novel *Look Homeward, Angel* didn't resonate so well with many residents in Wolfe's native Asheville who resented how they and their hometown were portrayed.

The resentment and cold shoulders from friends and family made it hard for him to go home. I certainly don't have that problem from my first book, but I think a lot of people who return home after a long absence find themselves navigating a defining line of who they were before they left and who they are now. We should be wiser and more secure than our younger selves.

I guess people who never leave don't have such a before-and-after contrast. There's no line in the sand. But probably, when anyone compares their 20-year-old self to their 50-year-old self, it's daunting. When we were young, mistakes were considered learning experiences, and we had endless years ahead of us to establish our "real life."

When we're older, married or divorced, wealthy or overdrawn, PBS or *Tiger King*, Gryffindor or Slytherin, Jordan or LeBron, some of us question if we took the right path. Did we try hard enough on the marriage or the degree or the children or the job?

"Lower your expectations" is a leading mantra for people of any age who feel they are coming up short of where they want to be. I had a good talk about all of this with my friend Margaret, who graduated from UNC with me.

"I think growing older is about self-acceptance. Some things won't change, and you need to be okay with that," she said. "Katherine, you are always going to text me before you visit and ask for my address, because you just don't update info in your phone and can barely decipher your messy address book. That's you. But that's not a serious flaw.

"And, when you survey your life at this point, you can't just take points off for what you don't like or haven't accomplished. You still have plenty of time to work on that. But you balance that with all you have done and what you do like about yourself and your life."

Margaret gains much of her wisdom from reading voraciously. Even in college, she had astute observations on life, yet her deep, hearty laugh—almost a cackle—back then and still now reveals she doesn't take herself too seriously.

My friend Penny, another confidant since college, offered sage words in her trademark Rocky Mount way.

"Girrrrrl, you got this. I know it's hard, I do. But you've done hard before. Hard's got nothing on Katherine Snow Smith," she said. "You cry as much as you want 'til that mascara is all over my new white shirt. Then you wash your face and you keep going. You got this. You are loved."

I brought my uneasiness about not being fully grown up to my newest advisor, the therapist I started seeing in Raleigh after my father died.

"Give yourself some grace," she said. "I'm going to tell you that at the beginning and end of each session."

"And what exactly does that mean? What does 'give yourself grace' really mean?" I asked in my reporter tone, because I've heard the same words of wisdom from Oprah and Brené Brown and don't really understand. "Is grace just a get-out-of-jail-free card when I come up short?"

"It means you are human. You make mistakes. You made them when you were in college, and you're still going to make mistakes all these years later," she said. "The mistakes don't define you. Don't let them overshadow all you've accomplished, Katherine."

After a few sessions, I realized I could take her positive feedback seriously, because she also challenged me on other issues and spoke honestly.

So, during that first year back in North Carolina, I realized starting over or growing old is about adjusting to what has changed, accepting what won't change, doing your best to change what you want to change and appreciating what you don't need to change.

You can go home again, Thomas. Just be sure to consider your whole story, know it's not over yet, get a good therapist and pack some L'Oréal root cover-up.

— 2 —

If We Have Wine and Toilet Paper

*M*y first book, *Rules for the Southern Rulebreaker: Missteps & Lessons Learned*, came out in the summer of 2020. I'm sure this book by a no-name author would have sailed right to the top of the *New York Times* Best Sellers list had the pandemic not thwarted my very small publisher's publicity plans.

I somehow managed to lure more than 100 people to a launch party on Zoom hosted by Tombolo Books in St. Petersburg and 125 to another Zoom talk at Quail Ridge Books in Raleigh.

But I don't take this as a big compliment. By July 2020, people would tune into Zoom to watch paint dry for an excuse to drink with others. Lara, one of my photographer friends from the *Tampa Bay Times*, assembled a montage photo of about 12 colleagues in their own Hollywood Square with glasses of wine at their lips during my first Zoom book talk from St. Petersburg.

Close to 20 dear, brave and foolish souls hosted various

outdoor book signings on their back patios, driveways or standing 6 feet apart inside large living rooms. My friend and neighbor, Deann, went through the motions with the city of St. Petersburg and neighbors to get our brick-paved street circa 1922 closed to traffic so she could serve champagne and cake to 25 neighbors sitting in soccer chairs. That was the plan at least.

In this case, neither alcohol nor I was the main draw. It was Deann's cake. Her reputation for baking far exceeded mine for writing. Any mortal baker would have made a sheet cake with the top decorated to look like my violet and pink book jacket. Deann, however, is not mortal. She made a five-layer cake, with each layer a separate book stacked on the other. The edges were decorated to look like pages on three sides and the spine of my book on the fourth. Only the top layer showed the front cover.

In 2020, however, creating this masterpiece that makes the Cake Boss's concoctions look like they're from an Easy-Bake Oven and closing off a street with flashing barricades wasn't the hardest part of hosting my book party. An hour before guests were to assemble, the bottom dropped out of a dark cloud over 18th Avenue harder than a 12-pack falls from a paper sack.

"I'd be glad to move the party into my house in normal times, but we can't have 20 people all crammed together eating and drinking," Deann said when the rain started.

"I totally agree," I said. "We have to cancel it. All I really wanted was the cake anyway. Now I don't have to share."

"I knew it," she said. "I just wish we knew somebody with a big tent or a huge building."

And then I got an idea. An awful idea. A wonderful, awful idea. Not as devious as the Grinch's, but pretty bold.

"I just wrote a story on how so many more people are selling their signed baseballs and other collectibles to get extra money while they can't work. I interviewed Blake and Brett Kennedy from Kennedy Brothers Auctions. Their warehouse is huge, and it's set up with rows of chairs from when people used to go to auctions in person."

I heard about the Kennedys when I first moved to St. Petersburg. New friends referred casually to "a Kennedy wedding" or "going out on the Kennedys' boat."

I'd played it cool and choked down the saliva pooling in my mouth while wondering how the hell these people made it to exclusive nuptials in Palm Beach or boarded 40-foot clippers in Hyannis.

Once I met a few of St. Petersburg's four Kennedy brothers and their wives, I learned there was no relation to the storied family, as well as no need for one. These Kennedys had just as much wit and warmth and far less scandal. As the rain poured on 18th Avenue, I texted Brett.

"I totally understand if you say no, but is there any way I could have 25 or so masked women come to the auction warehouse in 45 minutes for a book party?" I asked.

"It's fine with me but I'm at Palm Island," he replied. "Ask Blake. He's working today."

I didn't know his twin brother as well or even have his cell number, but I didn't earn the title of my first book being subtle and demure.

"Hey Blake. It's Katherine Snow Smith. This is a big ask, so blame Brett for giving me your number. I wrote this book and was going to have a party outside for it, but now it's pouring rain. Could we assemble about 20 women, a giant cake and some wine at the auction house in the next 30 minutes?"

"Come on over," he texted right back. "I was just about to leave, but I'm turning the lights back on."

Deann sent a "change of location" email to the partygoers, and I put all the wine into her car while her teenage sons loaded the fragile cake. We arrived at the 8,000-square-foot warehouse to find four rows of chairs 6 feet apart from each other.

"We aim to please," Blake said. "And my wife told me to buy three copies of your book." He tried three times to pay me even when I said no since he had made the party possible.

The way we threw everything together within 20 minutes reminded me of my high school days.

It was easy to pull off a last-minute party back in those days. My friends and I could congregate in Stuart Lindley's basement within 10 minutes of his parents' leaving the house for dinner. We'd play a cutthroat game of quarters, down three bags of Doritos, clean up all the evidence and be gone before Mr. and Mrs. Lindley even finished their dessert.

But the last-minute book party was more of an ode to Judy Tilson, the mother of Ann, who was one of my good friends since middle school.

"As long as we have wine and toilet paper, we can have a party," I heard Mrs. Tilson say on numerous occasions in my youth. She loved opening their stone house on Cowper Drive in Raleigh to friends, her kids' friends, and nonprofits ranging from the NC Symphony to Friends of the Library.

The Tilsons—Judy, her husband Hugh and their four kids—operated differently than other families I knew in Raleigh.

While their stately home in Hayes Barton, one of Raleigh's oldest neighborhoods, was furnished with the requisite antiques, from needlepointed dining room chairs to a walnut sideboard more than a century old, their family room featured something akin to wooden crates. The furniture was called This End Up and was made by some students at North Carolina State University. The Tilsons were early customers eager to support the venture and have furniture their kids and dogs could get dirty.

When we all slept over at the Tilsons' house, we had to be home by midnight. Ann would yell, "We're home," in the direction of her parents' room, then we'd walk right back out the door and rejoin the party we just left. If there was no party, we went to the kitchen for a late-night snack of asparagus wrapped in bacon, mini quiches or whatever was left over from the most recent fundraiser the Tilsons hosted.

If the refrigerator was bare, we'd order Domino's and, for some reason, throw the pizza box out of Ann's second-story bedroom window. The next morning, Mrs. Tilson would knock on the door and say, "You girls can go back to bed in a minute, but you need to go get that pizza box and put it in the garbage right now."

She wasn't mad. She didn't ask why we had the nerve to do such a thing. And she didn't seem to hold it against us.

(At my house, nobody came calling after 10 p.m. and certainly not a stranger bringing a pizza at midnight.)

Back in seventh grade, Ann wore a T-shirt picturing a cool illustration of a row of hands clapping. Her mom had handed it to her one morning when there was no clean laundry. The Tilson kids did their own laundry starting around sixth grade, so when someone's dresser ran dry, they borrowed from a sibling or relied on the giveaway

T-shirts from nonprofits their parents supported.

The caption under the clapping hands on Ann's shirt read: "Zap the Clap."

"Oh my God," she blurted out in a hushed tone with teeth clenched during study hall. "Guess what 'Zap the Clap' means."

"What?" I asked.

"Stop chlamydia."

"What's chlamydia?"

"Some kind of venereal disease people get from sex," she said. "A guy in second period just asked me if I had it. My mom must have gotten it from the health department. I hate my mom sooooooo much."

She wore the shirt wrong-side-out the rest of the day and berated her mother at dinner that night.

Mrs. Tilson brushed off her daughter's embarrassment as dramatic overreacting.

"Ann. People have to talk about sex and STDs openly to prevent unwanted pregnancies and venereal diseases. Grow up," she said.

My parents talked openly at our dinner table about everyone's day at work or school, politics, funny moments and other observations, but chlamydia and sex were not on the menu.

I didn't tell them about Ann's shirt, the pizza boxes out the window or that the Tilsons never locked their door in case somebody forgot their key. I didn't want my more conventional parents to have any reservations about Ann's upbringing. I certainly didn't want to be barred from her sleepovers.

But after our family went to the Tilsons' annual wassail party, my parents were Tilson devotees.

Wassail—mulled cider with applejack brandy— gave the party its name, but it was about so much more. The dining room table sagged with at least 20 cakes made by Mrs. Tilson. Little kids decorated cookies at the kitchen table, teenagers clandestinely took tastes of the wassail, adults from their 20s to 90s met a new face or old friend at every turn. And the "Good Dog Martha," as all the Tilsons called their springer spaniel, unabashedly nibbled at the cakes and cookies with barely a second glance from the hosts.

"That Judy Tilson made all those cakes herself," my mom raved on the way home.

"She and Hugh register voters on the weekends. And Judy volunteers at half a dozen other places. They host exchange students from around the world, and she knows more about what was in the paper last week than I do," raved my dad, the editor at the aforementioned paper.

Oh yes. The exchange students. They gave Ann some good clout when we got to Needham Broughton High School. Somehow the Tilsons never hosted a girl. They also never hosted a boy who wasn't fabulously good looking and the star of the soccer team.

All the "cool" people at Broughton wanted to get close to Hans, Peter and Ralph. One path was through Ann's brother Max, two years our senior, and the other was through Ann herself. The older girls who wanted to get close to the most exotic boys at Broughton left no path untaken. They offered Ann and her friends rides home after school, bought us beer and saved us seats on the front bleachers at soccer games.

Through the exchange students and brother Max, I got to know a locally born boy on the soccer team who was two years older than I was. He smiled at me when we passed in the halls between classes and seemed to always sit next to me when we climbed in Max's Volkswagen van after a game. Yet, he never asked me out. He did, however, fondle my lingerie.

I spent many Saturday nights with Ann, then met my parents at church the following morning. On one particular Saturday evening, I brought in my little overnight bag and my sexy, navy blue corduroy Laura Ashley jumper with the requisite white slip to wear to church. I laid them on the arm of a This End Up chair in the Tilsons' family room for a minute to play with the Good Dog Martha then totally forgot about my wardrobe.

The next morning Max, exchange student Hans and my crush were watching MTV as Ann and I walked into the family room. My crush's left hand was resting on the wooden arm of the chair, mindlessly caressing my silky slip. I am sure he had no idea it was mine or that it was even a woman's undergarment. I think it was kind of like when toddlers like the feel of a smooth satin border of a blanket on their chin or the tag of a stuffed animal between their fingers.

Ann and I quickly left the room and doubled over with laughter and embarrassment in the kitchen. I missed church that day because I didn't have the guts to retrieve my clothes from his hand.

One never knew what would happen at the Tilson house. But you knew you were welcome. Kids, foreigners, friends, dogs, Domino's, the NC Symphony, Friends of the Library and even chlamydia could always join the crowd.

My friend Louise in St. Petersburg is not unlike Mrs. Tilson. She regularly opens her elegant, one-story home on a pie-shaped lot on the water to friends and friends of friends. Back in the day when the *St. Petersburg Times* published a "social column," Louise's parties were featured from time to time, including references to Peaches, her pot-bellied pig, who made her way confidently among the long taffeta and silk skirts. Louise gave a great party for the 70th birthday of her daughter's father. They parted long ago but are still extremely close.

About the time the police arrived to say the band was too loud, another guest suffered a heart attack. Louise was hit with a noise ordinance ticket as the guest was loaded into an ambulance.

"You live long enough and give enough parties, it's bound to happen," Louise said, as she picked up one of many dogs' poops and the band played on at a slightly lower decibel level.

I've also tried to regularly open my home to our family members of all ages, from sleepovers for 20 fifth graders to going away parties for longtime colleagues steadily leaving the *Tampa Bay Times* as the newspaper's financial struggles prompted sad departures.

After I got divorced, I moved to a 1960s ranch house on the open water of Tampa Bay. I had to be out of town when a favorite editor left a storied journalism career, but I insisted the party be at my house with the view. Several friends texted me the next day saying they loved the new house and were sorry they never ran into me at the party.

The reason I could afford the rental on a street where mansions had mostly replaced all the original homes was because it had never been updated. The gorgeous view of the water was seen through cloudy crank jalousie windows. My Shangri-la had no central air conditioning, just a window unit in each of the two bedrooms and a lot of sliding doors with rickety screens. Still, on a steamy Saturday in May 2018, 25 women assembled to watch the nuptials of Harry and Meghan. Many guests sipping champagne and nibbling scones with clotted cream sat on the speckled terrazzo floor since there weren't enough seats. It was also 20 degrees cooler than sitting on the furniture. Heat rises, you know. Our oversized mutt, Charlie, thought any woman sitting criss-cross-apple-sauce on the floor wanted him to settle on in. He moved through more laps that day than any dancer on a good night at the Mons Venus.

By the time the "I do's" were done, my guests were fanning themselves with magazines and patting their foreheads with wet cocktail napkins.

"We are officially closed for the season, just like the Vinoy and Don CeSar Hotels used to do before they had air conditioning," I announced as Meghan and Harry walked out of St. George's Chapel.

"You never close your house," my friend Tiffany said. "I remember when you ran out of dessert at your 40th birthday party, you brought out raw cookie dough. We stayed another hour or two."

So at my house, if we have wine, toilet paper *and* cookie dough, we can have a party. Oh, and good friends are a must on the list too.

PARENTS
SHOULD
BE SEEN
AND NOT
HEARD

— 3 —

Parents Should Be Seen and Not Heard

Two days into a four-day trip to New York City, my kids were testing my patience.

They weren't elementary school age, complaining about walking 20 blocks instead of taking a cab or staying too long at the Met. They always did both wholeheartedly.

They weren't preteens whining for overpriced American Girl doll clothes or books. My girls always came to New York with a certain amount of spending money they'd earned from yard sales and a little cash from grandparents and knew that was their limit. My son was content with a street pretzel and a bootleg DVD of *Madagascar* from Chinatown.

This time Wade was 19 and Charlotte was 23. Olivia, my oldest, couldn't make the trip, but she would have been right there with Wade and Charlotte second guessing almost everything I uttered in the Big Apple.

When I said "gracias" to a Mexican waiter, I was condescending.

At another restaurant, I asked for dressing on the side, then sent back my salad when it was the Titanic in vinaigrette. I was too demanding.

When Hugh Jackman walked out on stage at *The Music Man*, and I whispered, "There's Hugh Jackman," they looked at me with furrowed brows and frenetic hand motions to be quiet as if I was screaming at the top of my lungs.

My kids are fabulous, wonderful people of a generation that gives me hope. These are the kids who walk out of school in nationwide protests for stricter gun control. They don't raise eyebrows at a gay or trans friend, neighbor, colleague or celebrity. They care more about the environment than all the generations before them combined.

But as careful as they are not to disturb a coral reef or offend an Uber driver, they have no problem offending the woman who brought them into this world and was financing four days in New York City.

"IT'S. ALWAYS. MOM'S. FAULT," a friend of mine texted when I told her I seemed to be constantly drawing my children's ire.

Of course we aren't the first generation of parents to have some antiquated ways compared to our children's more evolved beliefs. Younger generations have spurred and supported momentous progress in our country. I welcome their influence and guidance in changing ways. I can learn from them.

But guess what? They can learn from me, too, once in a while. And even if I do something they find embarrassing that's not hurting anyone, do they have to call me out every time?

One mom I know tries to keep texts to her son at no more than two sentences max after he complained they were too long. I'm sure her asking him about his plans interfered with his TikTok time.

One father waited until the last possible second to tell his newly licensed son to "STOP!" as he was about to blow through a red light.

"Dad! You're such a control freak," he retorted. "There's nobody coming from the other direction anyway."

I recently heard actress Keri Russell say she shared her hit show *Felicity*, beloved by millions, with her 11-year-old daughter. Within less than one episode her offspring turned it off saying: "Ugh, Mom, it's so cringey," Russell recounted on *Jimmy Kimmel Live!* Almost all parents have similar stories.

"I take a Sharpie and write the date of when I buy running shoes on the side so I know when they are getting kind of old and I need to replace them," my friend Brad told me as he lifted his left shoe to reveal three little numbers etched in black on the side. I pictured dating my mascara with a Sharpie, since I tend to keep it much longer than the short three-month shelf life beauty experts advise on *The Today Show*. (Al Roker and I had no idea.)

Well, while I saw sheer genius, Brad's son saw sheer geekness, rolling his eyes saying, "Uggh. That's such a dad thing."

My parents annoyed and embarrassed me a lot. I wasn't in a generation or a household where children were seen but not heard. Still, I held my tongue on plenty of occasions.

My friend Raiford told me he did the same. His father was exhibit A for those funny Progressive Insurance commercials that coach new homeowners on how to keep from becoming their parents, he said.

"You know when the coach says, 'The waiter doesn't

need to know your name'? That was written about my father," Raiford said. "Every single time we sat down at a table, he put out his hand. 'Bill Garrabrant. Good to meet you.'"

Bill would go on to order a beer and a glass of ice.

"He felt it critical to explain to the waiter why he wanted ice in his beer," Raiford continued. "He'd say, 'You know, three wonderful things happen when you add ice to your beer. It turns high test beer into light beer, it turns 12 ounces into 16 ounces, and it keeps it cold.' He always said the same thing. Every time."

"So what would the waiters do? What would you do?" I asked.

"The waiter couldn't get away from the table fast enough. I guess I'd just look at my sister or brother and roll my eyes," Raiford recalled. "Then as I got older, and he got older, it didn't bother me. He liked saying it, and he wasn't hurting anyone."

Raiford now tries to be more like his father in his "never met a stranger" way.

As for my children, maybe, just maybe, they might try to emulate some of my annoying but harmless habits when they get older. For now, they will find fault with me, just as all children find fault with their parents at every age. But my kids also write me meaningful notes, hug me often and, I think, are more proud than pained by me. Once in a while, I even get a text longer than three sentences that isn't requesting money or their Social Security number.

I'll take it.

— 4 —

I Don't Make My Own Keys

I think of my elegant and forthright older friend Mary every time I'm at the grocery store choosing between a long checkout line with a human cashier or using the self-checkout option with no waiting.

"I don't pump my own gas, and I don't do cash bars," Mary often said, rarely under her breath, when we walked into a party that lacked an open bar. Mary worked as a reporter for 47 years at the *Tampa Bay Times*, where I worked for 20 years.

She crossed numerous gender barriers during her time as a reporter, was known for brushing off male bosses with whom she disagreed like lint from her St. John's knit suit, yet stuck to plenty of old-school female standards.

She might work 10-hour days scribbling notes and banging out stories, but her hands were not meant for gas pumps reeking of gasoline. She was meant for other pumps, in an array of colors.

"I'm changing into my heels when we get inside, but I brought flats for crossing Pasadena Boulevard because we're gonna have to haul ass," Mary would say as we parked across from Temple Bethel for the opening day of the annual art festival. Of course her hauling-ass shoes were still higher than the ones I wore to the actual event, and I was 35 years younger.

After covering various beats, she was the paper's community and social reporter, but her quick wit, warm ways and deep knowledge of all-things-St. Petersburg charmed business leaders and government officials just as they did debutantes and philanthropic donors. Everyone wanted to be Mary's friend. For every story she wrote on the opening of an exhibition at the Dalí Museum or the unveiling of the Manalo Blahnik line at Saks, Mary broke news or passed along tips about a local bank merger or big Republican donor who was about to be named a US ambassador.

It's not that Mary considered herself too good to pay at a cash bar or pump her own gas. These were evolutions that made life a little less dignified and added one more step to a process that used to be easier.

That's how I feel when it's 6:35 p.m. and I'm at Publix buying 15 items, (three too many to go through the express lane) and the shortest lines are at the self-checkout terminals. I'm not wearing my glasses so it's a pain to look up the code for grapes, and somehow, every time I weigh my bananas I ring in the higher price for the organic watermelon. If I'm also buying wine, seven alarms go off, and I have to wait for a cashier to strip search me before I can check out. Some sort of artificial intelligence facial recognition would most certainly speed up that process of discerning who is over 21.

Mary died one year into COVID-19 from another un-expected health issue. She was still in quarantine and never experienced the world of masked, contactless and automated living. Of course, we all miss her, but maybe the timing was right. Mary was all about connecting with people, from the man who pumped her gas to the newest reporter in the newsroom. She wasn't wired to live 6 feet apart or not squeeze hands and hug.

I thought of her again when I had to get an extra house key made recently and the cheerful salesman at Lowe's led me to a machine half the size of an ATM.

"Just follow the directions," he said. "It walks you right through it."

"Through what?"

"Through making the key."

"Wait. What?" I stammered. "I usually just hand it to someone who works here, and they make it."

"Not anymore. We started this during COVID. Now you put your key in this machine, then follow the directions to cut another one."

I have no problem pumping my own gas, but I'm not cutting my own key. I'm hanging on to a few luxuries left in life.

I drove to the local Ace hardware, which has yet to in-stall a self-serve key maker. As an employee cut my key, we chatted about time he lived in my native North Carolina. He was a marine at Camp Lejeune and a helicopter pilot during the Vietnam War. He recently beat prostate cancer that he thinks came from exposure to Agent Orange.

I left with a new key, no stress from making my own and an interesting story. I wish I could tell Mary all about it.

sno' foolin'

by A.C. Snow

— 5 —

Tales from the Newsroom

I was lucky to not only work in a newsroom for much of my life, but to grow up around one as well.

On slow news days, a feature on a high school spelling bee winner and a story on a one-cent sewer rate increase adorn the front page. Other times, a moment in history mobilizes every reporter, photographer and editor to cover a natural disaster or consequential election day. Whatever the day, newsrooms are never boring, nor are the people who inhabit them.

Many workplaces, whether action-packed or mundane, are filled with camaraderie that brings colleagues closer than family. Coworkers at hospitals, law enforcement agencies, fire departments and in the military deal with life and death daily. Their shared experiences create bonds the rest of us can't fathom.

But whatever the nature of the job, people who work together form a special connection. There's plenty of proof in beloved TV shows like *The Office, Parks and Recreation, Cheers* and *The Mary Tyler Moore Show*.

The shared experiences in newsrooms are distinctive perhaps because they are so pointedly marked by the highs and lows of the city, state and nation we cover, along with the highs and lows in our own lives. News organizations also tend to attract inquisitive, extroverted people with conflicting doses of hope and cynicism, humor and heartache. We have a shared task of serving, and sometimes standing up to, a public that both derides us and relies on us.

My father was a reporter and then editor-in-chief of *The Raleigh Times*, the city's afternoon paper that closed in 1989 around the time hundreds of other afternoon papers across the country became redundant because cable news channels offered nonstop coverage. After that, he continued to write his public interest column for the morning paper, *The News & Observer*, until he was 95.

One of Daddy's favorite stories illustrating the relationship between newspapers and the public centered on an overpriced ham biscuit. He was working late one night in the early '80s, and a woman visiting Raleigh from a few counties east somehow walked right past the guard's desk in the lobby, took the elevator to the third floor and found her way to his office.

"Mr. Snow. I ask you. Do you think it's right for an establishment to charge $1.95 for a ham biscuit that has no more ham than this?" she asked, unwrapping tinfoil to expose a skimpy piece of ham between two golden bookends. "I believe we should be able to visit our state's capital, eat in a local restaurant and receive more fair treatment. Surely you can do something about this."

I was reminded of the ham biscuit incident at *The*

Raleigh Times many years later when I was working as a reporter at the *Tampa Bay Times*. Dolly, our warm and patient news clerk whose phone was the gateway between the public and the paper, tried to placate a caller as she looked over a full-page Delta Air Lines ad featuring a scene from a faraway land.

"It definitely looks like the Great Wall of China to me, ma'am, but I can't say for sure. I agree it would be nice if there was a line explaining where it is," she said to the irate subscriber. "But we didn't make this ad. Delta sent it to us this way. ... Yes, I completely understand your frustration."

She also fielded calls from people who'd lost a job, lost a dog or couldn't find their way to the emergency room. Newspapers were the first line of defense for many.

My father embraced email exchanges when they eclipsed the phone calls, personal visits and handwritten letters. One of his favorites reached his in-box after his updated photo ran in the paper.

"I see you have a new photo at the top of your column. I used to come downtown and see you drinking coffee with your friends at the Professional Pharmacy," the reader wrote. "You were ugly as hell then, and you're ugly as hell now."

And then there were calls from the clients who paid for those ads that kept the presses running. My father told me about another time back in the '70s when a disgruntled client didn't like how his ad looked in the paper and called to complain to one of the top ad men.

"I need to speak to Ike Schwartz right away," he said to the receptionist.

"I'm sorry, Mr. Schwartz isn't in. Could I take a message?" she asked.

"Well, when will he be back? I need to get my ad fixed before it runs again tomorrow," the caller demanded.

"I'm sorry. Mr. Schwartz will be out all day. This is Yom Kippur," she replied.

"Well, Yom, I guess you're just going to have to help me get this thing right," he said.

Decades later, my colleagues in the *Tampa Bay Times'* 10-person Pasco County bureau laughed over another "lost in translation" situation between a reporter and researcher. Before the Internet allowed reporters to check public records and dive deep into any topic on our own, we relied heavily on newspapers' research departments. When the Clyde Beatty-Cole Bros. Circus came to rural Pasco County in 1995, it was big local news to have a big-top performance come to the more rural neighbor of Tampa and St. Petersburg. Roger, a colleague covering the coming attraction, asked the research department to peruse the microfiche and periodicals for history of the Clyde Beatty Circus.

An hour later, the researcher sent the reporter 10 reviews of actor Warren Beatty's performance in *Bonnie and Clyde*.

The newsroom howled.

The Pasco County bureau was a first stop for many new reporters, some of whom would go on to be White House correspondents, Pulitzer winners and reporters or editors at some of the country's top news organizations. The success rate was largely due to an editor named Mike Moscardini, who was extremely tough on reporters but pushed them to be better. He also had a great, cynical sense of humor.

Even if you had worked three 12-hour days in a row, anyone leaving work before 6 p.m. received his standard parting words: "Well, thanks for stopping by."

He often stood at his desk, where he kept about a dozen rubber ducks in a row, and gazed at the newsroom to single out a reporter. "Katherine. What have you done today to make me look good in the eyes of my superiors?"

One Friday, a group of us went to a restaurant for a lunch that took almost two hours because of slow service. When the waiter brought the checks and offered the token "Have a nice weekend," Moscardini quipped, "Yeah. What's left of it."

While we were used to covering bizarre Florida crimes in our daily section called "The Pasco Times," a few members of the newsroom themselves got arrested all within the course of a week. First, a general assignment reporter without a car, and apparently without a calendar as well, failed to return his rental and was arrested for grand theft of an auto. Then, a sports reporter was charged with disorderly conduct after fighting with a neighbor. Finally, another reporter received a disturbing-the-peace charge during a heated argument with his wife.

After the third staffer clashed with the law, Moscardini stood at his desk to announce: "We're changing our name from 'The Pasco Times' to 'The Doin' Times.'"

"Oh, and everybody has to get new photos taken for their columns," he decreed. "We're going to start running a head shot and your profile."

Journalists play pranks.

A crime reporter at the *Tampa Bay Times* once covered the police raid of a "sexual fantasy fulfillment room" that included whips, chains, human skulls and fur-covered handcuffs. (The owner, who was charged with prostitution and racketeering, pointed out the cuffs were self-releasing so nobody was forced into anything.) The day after the story ran, an editor handed the crime reporter an official look-ing printout explaining the authorities had released a list of regular customers. It included the name of the paper's managing editor and his correct home address. The list was a fake. But the reporter had no idea and had to confront the editor, who also was not in on the joke. Everyone else in the newsroom was in on it and watched the awkward confron-tation through the glass window of the editor's office.

A photographer and a reporter at *The Raleigh Times* played a prank on my father, their editor, in 1984. The pair was on downtown Raleigh's Fayetteville Street Mall asking passersby for their opinion on the ousting of Vanessa Wil-liams as Miss America after *Penthouse* magazine published nude photos taken long before she was crowned. My father happened to pass them on his way to a meeting, and the reporter handed him the centerfold to peruse. By the time Daddy got back to the newspaper office, photos of the ed-itor-in-chief gazing at *Penthouse* were posted throughout the building.

Years ago, I took my kids to the mostly empty *Tampa Bay Times* newsroom on a Sunday to play a prank on their ol' dad. Adam had been on the road for two weeks straight, and this was long before FaceTime or Zoom. I wanted the kids to feel connected to him. Olivia, Charlotte and Wade, all under the age of 10, giggled as we greased Adam's pens, drawer handles and phone receiver with Vaseline. Olivia had the honor of taking the ball out of his computer mouse to render it inoperable. Back at home, we laughed every time we pictured Adam's surprise when he returned to the office in a few days.

Turns out, he wasn't the first person to sit at his desk. His boss, Tim, was editing a story over the phone with

Adam and needed to pull up a file from his computer. He transferred the call to Adam's desk.

"There's like weird crap all over your phone," Tim groused. "What have you been eating?"

Adam later shared the rest of the conversation with us.

"Your mouse isn't working. It does nothing," Tim complained.

"Go in my top drawer, I think I have another one," a clueless Adam replied.

"This same stuff is all over your drawers. What are you doing here, man?" Tim asked.

"I don't know what you're talking about," Adam replied.

"What the hell? All of your pens are covered in this slime too," Tim said. "How do you work like this?"

To me, it's just as funny twenty years later, but maybe you had to be there.

Fortunately, I was there—in a newsroom. In person. Long before they became remote, hybrid or were reduced to a shadow of what they once were because slashed budgets shredded staff.

I'll always appreciate those years and miss them. Funny how the stress, deadlines, boring stories and pit-in-your-stomach, yearning-to-immediately-evaporate feeling that comes with an error in print once every few years aren't as memorable now.

— 6 —

Firsts

First kiss. First concert. First car. First flight. First foreign country.

Life is full of firsts. Not everyone remembers the same list of these primary moments in their lives because each one carries different weight for different people.

I can recall many of my classic firsts, but I may be one of the few people who can remember her first thong. It wasn't my own, but one worn by a coworker at *The Charlotte Business Journal* back when panty lines were an accepted way of life and floss was threaded only between teeth.

That first thong occurred one Friday afternoon in 1992, when everyone from work went bowling for some mandatory team-building outside of the office. We were a small staff, and all seemed to get along relatively well even without the forced field trip. Nine of us, including two editors, were on the news side, three people in production designed the paper, and seven sales reps brought in the money with advertising and circulation.

A woman named Tammy who could have passed for Rapunzel sold subscriptions and sat behind me. She was about 40, had three kids and seemed ancient to my 24-year-old self. Still we'd roll our chairs back to chat from time to time when our bosses weren't watching. When I left after two years to get married and move to Florida, Tammy signed my going-away card with "back-door neighbors are best." I love that phrase.

But, back to that first thong. Spoiler alert: It wasn't Tammy's.

"Someone here isn't wearing any underwear." The whisper from the glossed lips of a classified ad salesperson passed to someone in production who passed it onto someone in display ads and then to someone in news. Once the baton passed to me, I rushed to bond with the closest coworker and whispered the shocking revelation in her ear.

"I don't know who it is. But apparently someone here isn't wearing underwear. She has white pants and no panty lines," I said.

"It's called a thong," the thin woman in finance snapped. I suddenly noticed she was wearing white pants with no panty lines. "It's regular underwear in the front and like dental floss in the back," she said "I can't believe this!"

This woman clearly was doing nothing worth gossiping about—even if it had been no underwear and not a thong. She was actually at the forefront of fashion.

I still cringe remembering that moment. Not just because I was caught, but because I joined the flock and passed on the gossip. But, that was my first thong.

Other firsts are better memories. My first flight was in second grade when my family flew to Washington, DC, for my father's annual American Society of Newspaper Editors conference. Minutes after we took off, my sister, in fifth grade at the time, asked why there were little white bags in every seat. She threw up in one as my mother explained.

My first concert was Prince with Sheila E. opening when I was a sophomore in high school. Mic drop.

My first car was a used 1977 white Ford Mustang my junior year in high school. My father found it in the classifieds, paid for it as well, and it was the best first car a girl could love. Maroon interior. Stick shift. And a "moon roof" that weighed about 200 pounds and was easily lifted out of the top of the Mustang by a team of four high school girls using all our might, then stowed in a faux leather case in the trunk.

My first foreign country was an exotic land called "the United Kingdom." I somehow made it there without any incident for a summer study-abroad program in college. Before we left Chapel Hill, the two professors for the annual summer trip aired "Midnight Express."

It scared the hell out of us, and nobody tried to transport drugs to or from a foreign country. Perhaps we would have also benefited from a crash course in the language barrier in London, or lack thereof. A couple hours after landing at Gatwick, five friends and I ate our first European lunch at an exotic spot called "Pizza Hut." One friend ordered a "Co-Ca-Col-A" in slow motion and loudly so the waitress would understand her foreign tongue.

"I got you, honey," the English waitress responded.

My first kiss is a longer memory than most of my firsts. I was in eighth grade and Collier was in ninth. It was in the early '80s when boys were still asking girls, "Will you go with me," as they sat next to each other in the cafeteria or lingered around lockers after school. Collier, who was mature for his 15 years, realized this was cliché.

We had talked and flirted for a month or two around the soccer field, between classes and after school. One afternoon he boldly said he liked me but thought asking me to "go together" sounded kind of dumb. Had he been a smooth operator with tally marks of discarded girls and broken hearts I might have worried he was trying to play some kind of ninth grade game with me. But Collier was a good guy. Smart, funny, a little on the quiet side. I agreed we didn't need to conform to immature junior high labels.

After we had officially expressed our feelings without officially "going together," we talked on the phone every night and walked hand in hand between classes at Daniels Junior High School. My eyes became attuned to spotting his green Izod windbreaker in the crowded halls.

After a couple weeks of courtship, we made plans for him and a friend to stop by my friend Beth McConnell's house, where a few girls and I were spending a Friday night. At first, we hung in the game room playing foosball and watching TV with everyone else. Then Collier and I slipped into Beth's room. The others pretended not to notice our exit, but within seconds of that first kiss we heard some clapping and laughter. Collier and I looked out the window and saw a row of onlookers out in the yard.

A few weeks later, school was over, and since I was soon leaving for summer camp, we decided it was best to part ways. Since we had never "gone together" we didn't have to break up. After that, Collier went away to boarding school. We talked a few times when we crossed paths in subsequent years.

I had not seen Collier in more than a year when he died in a car accident the summer after his sophomore year at

Davidson College. As sad as I was, it goes without saying and I was and am light-years away from feeling the pain his family and close friends suffered and still feel.

I will say that in college when the subject of first kisses came up among girls drinking Natural Lights and I said mine was a boy named Collier, anyone who knew him smiled and said he was such a fun, kind and sincere person.

A few years after he died, during my first job when I started going to the banks regularly to deposit my paychecks, I noticed those plastic tubes at the drive-throughs were marked with the manufacturer's name: Collier Safe Company. So for more than 30 years, every time I'm at a bank and see "Collier" stamped on shiny silver equipment, I picture Collier in his green windbreaker.

A verse by Scottish Poet Thomas Campbell from his 1825 poem "Hallowed Ground" is etched on Collier's gravestone. It gives me comfort when I think of him and other special people I miss.

"To Live in Hearts We Leave Behind Is Not To Die."

— 7 —

Janet Reno's Peacock Party

Long before Instagram was the accepted vehicle for proud parents to post their kids' first steps, sports victories, school play curtain calls and acceptance emails from colleges, we competed via class pets and Flat Stanley. Photos of the family and Flat Stanley skiing in Park City or the stuffed animal that served as the class mascot on the Disney Magic cruise ship were a rudimentary form of Instagram back when the Internet was just a twinkle in Al Gore's eye.

Google "Flat Stanley celebrities" and you'll find countless images of famous people holding the outline of a paper doll decorated with the uneven crayon strokes of a 7-year-old. Presidents George W. Bush, Bill Clinton and Barack Obama smile broadly with various versions of Flat Stanley. Sarah Jessica Parker, Buzz Aldrin, Clint Eastwood and Jon Stewart are also among the celebs happily posing for photos with Flat Stanley.

The so-called Flat Stanley Project started as a way to make young readers interested in a book about a boy accidentally squashed by a bulletin board who could be sent through the mail to anywhere in the world. Students read the book, made their own versions of Flat Stanley and kept a photographic journal of their experiences together. Plenty of Stanleys made mundane rounds to the grocery store, church or Taco Bell, while others traveled the world and met luminaries, thanks to parents who wanted to make sure their child's Stanley was the most interesting feature in the class's year-end photo album.

For my first child, it wasn't a Flat Stanley paper doll, but a well-worn stuffed animal named Petey the Peacock who went home with a different kindergartner each week. By the time Olivia proudly brought Petey into our home, the stuffed animal had dined at the Eiffel Tower, seen the changing of the guard at Buckingham Palace and sat behind Spike Lee at a Lakers game.

We were lucky enough to have Petey during a visit to see grandparents in Connecticut. Olivia was thrilled to get photos of Petey with the airplane pilot, Petey in the kitchen with her grandparents and Petey on a stone deer statue in their backyard. She decided the mission was complete. However, her dad and I worried this would pale next to the snapshot of Petey with Tom Hanks or in the DMZ between the two Koreas.

Our family returned from Connecticut on Saturday night, and Adam left early the next morning to report on Janet Reno's campaign for Florida's governor. Reno was revered by some and abhorred by others.

The Miami native and former attorney general under President Clinton had earned bad reviews as the overseer of the botched raid on cult leader David Koresh that resulted in the deaths of more than 70 Branch Davidians in

Waco, Texas. She also orchestrated the heartbreaking and no-win seizure of 5-year-old Elián González from his dead mother's Florida family so he could return to his father in Cuba.

Still, Reno was admired by many. She was the country's first female attorney general, one of 16 female graduates from Harvard Law School in 1963 and a tough Miami prosecutor. Reno grew up on the edge of the Everglades in a house her mother built out of cypress and brick. She achieved pop culture fame when Will Ferrell portrayed her on *Saturday Night Live* as a tough-talking government official with a surprisingly lighter side hosting dance parties in her basement. Reno even appeared on the show to poke fun at herself and dance with Ferrell. They wore matching royal blue dresses.

I was cutting smiley faces into the cheese quesadillas for the girls' dinner when Adam called.

"Janet Reno is making a surprise appearance in St. Petersburg at that new gay resort near the beach. Can you get Olivia and that stuffed peacock there in 20 minutes?" he asked. "I bet there's no other picture of him with a U.S. attorney general."

When we pulled up to the hotel, at least 10 TV trucks from Tampa, St. Petersburg, Orlando and Sarasota flanked the entrance of the hotel. The camera crews already had plenty of footage of men in tank tops and shorts cheering for Reno, so when a pregnant woman carrying a toddler and holding the hand of a pensive 5-year-old girl gripping a green and blue stuffed peacock came on the scene, all cameras turned on us.

Oh yeah. I forgot until I looked back at the photos. I was five months pregnant with that third child.

"Mommy, why are all these cameras here?" Olivia asked as we walked into the hotel.

"Janet Reno is very famous," I said. "And Florida has never had a woman governor so it's a big deal. You don't need to talk to them. We're just going to say hello to Ms. Reno."

The former attorney general was chatting up the crowd but paused when she saw this little girl with blonde Shirley Temple curls come into the crowd.

"Hello, Ms. Reno. We are so happy to have a woman like you running for governor," I said. "This is Olivia and her class mascot Petey the Peacock. Can I get a picture of you with them?"

"Certainly. Olivia, thank you for coming tonight and bringing Petey. Did you know I grew up with peacocks all around me?" Reno asked, as Olivia released my hand and moved closer to Reno.

"No. I did not know that," she said.

"Well, when I was a little girl like you, peacocks lived all around my house. Most of them still live there," Reno continued.

"How many peacocks do you have?" Olivia asked.

"Oh, around 20 or so. They aren't pets like a dog or a cat, but they will come right up to me on our porch or in the yard, " the candidate explained, speaking only to Olivia and not the cameras. "They're spectacular."

"Spectacular?" Olivia was now leaning against Reno's lap while the candidate held Petey.

"Yes. Do you know what spectacular means?"

"Really great?"

"That's exactly right, Olivia."

Reno lost the Democratic primary to Tampa attorney Bill McBride, who went on to lose to Jeb Bush.

Janet Reno is probably not the most famous person Petey ever met. But that exchange between the legendary woman and young Olivia was nothing short of spectacular.

— 8 —

On the Campaign Trail

For two decades, my children's lives, as well as mine, were punctuated by the local, state and national politics Adam covered.

My son Wade broke his arm at age 7 jumping off an ornamental rock sculpture in St. Petersburg's Straub Park when we went downtown to join Adam as he covered a speech by gubernatorial candidate Kendrick Meek. Two years later, I took Olivia, Charlotte and Wade to see their father moderate the 2012 Republican presidential debate with NBC's Brian Williams in Tampa. The whole way home, as the clock neared midnight on a school night, they lamented how their father, along with Mitt Romney, Newt Gingrich and Rick Santorum didn't let that "sweet old doctor"—Ron Paul—talk as much as the others.

As the kids reached middle school and formed political opinions of their own, they weren't allowed to put campaign stickers on their notebooks or cheer for candidates at political rallies. We all had to appear neutral because of their father's job.

We have photos of one, two or all three kids with Florida governors Lawton Chiles, Jeb Bush and Charlie Crist, as well as Sen. Bill Nelson, now the head of NASA. They've met presidential candidates including Romney, John Kerry, John McCain, John Edwards, Hillary Clinton and Rudy Giuliani.

I recently found a stack of old kitchen calendars filled with Adam's travel dates, which outline the anatomy of a presidential campaign in a rainbow of Sharpies.

Eighteen months before each presidential election, from 2000 to 2016, Adam spent a week or so in Des Moines, Iowa, along with every national political reporter and presidential hopeful. The Iowa State Fair is a right of passage for political contenders. They woo the country's first voters by shaking hands, kissing babies and taking selfies with a life-size sculpture of a cow made out of butter.

Adam would then go back to Iowa the following January for the state's primary, which Iowa calls a caucus. From there he'd fly straight to New Hampshire to cover candidates campaigning a week before its primary, then after the Granite State voted, the press and politicians spent another week in South Carolina for its primary. In March, the field narrowed to a candidate for each party and perhaps an independent. Adam was only on the road for a night or two when a frontrunner campaigned somewhere in Florida. In late summer he was gone again for a couple weeks to attend each party's national convention. Finally, by election night, he was home for good.

Well, except in 2000. That year, Adam came home from the downtown St. Petersburg newsroom around 3 a.m. after it seemed George W. Bush won the nailbiter.

I turned on *The Today Show* four hours later.

"Adam! Wake up," I said as he slept next to me. "They're recounting Florida. Gore isn't conceding. What's a chad?"

In less than an hour, he was driving to South Florida, and we didn't see him again until Thanksgiving.

Unlike the families of parents who are gone for months and years at a time serving in the military, we were lucky to enjoy the occasional perk of tagging along with Adam when he traveled for work.

These trips took us to nice hotels on the newspaper's dime and brought unexpected encounters as well.

One year, we joined him in Miami for the annual Jefferson-Jackson Dinner. While Adam was on break between speeches and schmoozing, the whole family hit Lincoln Road for lunch and people-watching at what was then the eclectic, edgy retail strip of South Beach. We stopped in an art gallery that was going out of business and bought a deeply discounted painting of palm fronds in an array of about 20 shades of green on a 5-foot-by-5-foot canvas.

Adam had to rush off to cover something as soon as we returned to the hotel. Since the gallery owner had warned us not to leave the painting in our trusty Honda Odyssey minivan because the heat would ruin it, I dragged it into the hotel, pushed Wade in the stroller and directed Olivia, age 7, to corral her 5-year-old sister and push the elevator button to our room.

"You got your hands full," a man in the elevator said. He was sandwiched against the wall with Wade, the stroller and me while Olivia and Charlotte were on the other side of the painting that rudely divided the elevator.

I recognized his voice before I looked at his face and realized the man I cornered with my discounted art was political strategist James Carville.

"It's the economy, stupid," I blurted out more than a decade after he coined the iconic phrase when advising Bill Clinton's first presidential run.

He offered a slight laugh.

"I'm sorry. I'm sure you get sick of hearing that," I mumbled as I cringed.

"I see you're really attached to that painting," Carville said, nodding at the canvas that barely fit in the elevator.

"We take it everywhere we go. I just like to make a hotel room feel like home," I said.

"Not a thing in the world wrong with that," he replied.

From then on, Adam and I referred to this palm frond painting as being part of "The Carville Collection."

Lucky for the kids, Walt Disney World was the most frequent destination where we joined Adam on the road. No matter the candidate, the party, the race or the age, gender or cultural demographic of supporters, the majority of political events seemed to take place within three or fewer miles of the House of Mouse.

We crowded into free hotel rooms so often, in fact, that my parents started giving us annual Disney passes for Christmas. My mom loved buying one thing that was easy to wrap and lasted all year long.

One time, the children and I drove straight to the Magic

Kingdom and spent the day at the park while Adam, who was already in Orlando, covered whatever political event was taking place. He met us in front of Cinderella's castle late in the afternoon, but by that time young Wade had been at the ball way too long. I gave Adam the car keys, got his room key and went back to the hotel with Wade via the monorail.

When we arrived, I realized all our luggage was in the car in the Magic Kingdom parking lot and Adam wasn't driving the girls to the hotel until after the 10 p.m. fireworks. Fine. No big deal. We'd just sleep in our clothes, and I'd buy a pack of Pull-Ups at the hotel shop.

After paying about $50 for eight diapers—that damn mouse gets you coming and going—I took 18-month-old Wade to the hotel's cafe, the least expensive option, for dinner.

Unfortunately, it was next to the pool, and once that sweaty little boy saw the crystal blue water, he wanted nothing more than to go for a splash. I tried to explain we didn't have our swimsuits and that we'd have no dry clothes to change into until his father and sisters got to the hotel in several hours. He kept looking longingly at the pool and all its waterfalls and tiered hot tubs.

"You know what, Wade? Life is short," I relented. "We'll just swim in our clothes."

I cherish the memory of wading into the pool in my white jeans and flowered tunic with Wade in his T-shirt and shorts. After our glorious rule-breaking swim, we went to the hotel room. I hung up our wet clothes in the bathroom, tucked him into one king-sized bed wearing just his pricey Pull-Up, then settled into the other in my birthday suit. We were cozy and content, watching *Curious George*, when I heard the door open, and suddenly a man I'd never seen in my life walked in pulling a suitcase.

"Get out," I screamed, clutching the 400-thread-count comforter up around my neck.

"This is *my* room," the startled intruder yelled back.

"Get out. Get the hell out right now. I'm calling 9-1-1," I said, reaching for the phone, trying not to expose myself.

"I'm leaving. I'm sorry. But this is my room," the 30-something stranger said as he retreated.

"Who dat, Mommy?" Wade asked.

"I do not know. But he's gone and we're fine," I answered, trying not to alarm him more than my screaming already did.

The phone rang.

"Hello. This is Jessica at the front desk. May I ask your name?" the voice on the line said.

"Katherine Snow Smith. This room is in my husband's name, Adam Smith," I answered as calmly as possible.

"Thank you, Mrs. Smith. Um, uhhh. Thank you. Your husband is in the lobby and would like to check into the room," Jessica stammered, thinking she was in the middle of quite the messed-up marital spat.

"That man is not my husband. I have never seen him in my life," I said. "He just walked right into my room. You need to call the police immediately if he's saying he's my husband."

"Mrs. Smith, he showed me identification confirming he is Adam Smith and has a room reservation," Jessica countered.

"Well, maybe there's more than one Adam Smith in the world, or at least at this hotel," I said. "Check your records, and you'll see another Adam Smith checked in two days ago."

Turns out the terrified Adam Smith standing before her was a young Republican operative from Tampa who was handed the key for the room of Adam Smith, political editor from St. Petersburg, who checked in the day before.

Once the mystery was unraveled, Jessica apologized profusely and offered me two vouchers to the "deluxe" Sunday brunch the next day.

"Well, there are five of us, so if you can come up with three more vouchers, you got yourself a deal," I said.

This was not the only time I suffered a wardrobe malfunction in political circles. I've already mentioned the time I fell on Barack Obama during a photo opp at a White House Christmas Party. (I probably should not have borrowed 4-inch heels for the occasion.)

Another shoe mishap occurred when my sister Melinda and I joined our parents at a White House reception for the American Society of Newspaper Editors during Gerald Ford's presidency in 1977. I was 9 and insisted on packing for myself. My mother allowed it, though she made sure to put my neatly pressed, long, ruffled, green-and-white gingham dress in her hanging bag. Upon unpacking in Washington, DC, we realized Little Miss Independent failed to bring her black patent leather shoes.

Only once I was a mother myself could I understand the frustration my own mother must have felt when we went through the receiving line to meet Gerald and Betty Ford with me clomping around in well-worn Keds.

As the executive editor of the afternoon paper, my father didn't travel out of town too often, but did share stories of a few memorable moments on the campaign trail.

He was once in a buffet line behind one of North Carolina's governors at the Carolina Inn in Chapel Hill after the politician made a speech. A server behind a chafing dish doled out a piece of crispy fried chicken to each person. The governor asked for a second piece, and she said she was sorry but it was just one per person.

"Do you know who I am?" the politician replied. "I'm the governor. I'm in charge of this whole state."

"Do you know who I am?" the server countered. "I'm Clarice. And I'm in charge of chicken. One piece per person."

"Everybody needs to be in charge of something," Daddy told me after recounting the incident years later.

My father was with another North Carolina elected official at an event when a woman — perhaps a long-ago friend or recent donor — came up to the politician with her hand covering her nametag.

"Do you know my name?" she asked excitedly.

"It's so good to see you," he said warmly with a sturdy handshake.

"Tell me what my name is," she persisted. "Just say my name."

The politician, realizing there was no easy way out, grew frustrated and looked at the crowd around him.

"Could somebody please tell this poor woman who she is. She seems to have no idea."

Daddy had another favorite story from the era when politicians weren't so careful about curating a perfect public image. He was once with one governor at his family home in rural North Carolina. The governor strode down to the end of the long front porch and pointed to a dead patch in the lawn. He explained with a laugh that no grass grew there because that's where he relieved himself when he didn't want to leave the outdoors and go inside to the bathroom.

When my father started at *The Raleigh Times*, he covered the city council, which included a 30-something Jesse Helms, who was a Democrat at the time, as well as a former newspaper reporter. The politician, who went on to be an iconic leader in the conservative movement as a United States senator from 1973 to 2003, opposed civil rights, gay rights, environmentalism, abortion, affirmative action and most every other liberal platform. My father vigorously opposed Helms's positions in editorials, and needless to say, the paper never endorsed him.

Yet, the two were amiable. They saw each other as fathers and husbands and hardworking people and not just political polar opposites. They treated each other with respect.

My parents were out of the country when my sister died. Their answering machine was full when they got home. Helms left the first message, offering his and his wife Dot's condolences. He made a donation to the SPCA in her honor. A decade later when the former senator was in his final years at a Raleigh retirement home, my father visited him from time to time.

Politics is not for the faint of heart, whether you're a politician or the press. But as with most jobs, honesty and humor go a long way.

I saw my former husband walk a balanced line the best he could as well. Adam could have a sharp tongue and short fuse but was also a very thorough and fair reporter. And he was recognized for that fairness by the people he covered.

We joined him at some convention, rally or speech in the late 1990s, when he first introduced us to Janet Reno.

She shook hands with Olivia and said: "Your father is a very tough reporter but also extremely fair."

Ten minutes later, Adam introduced us to Bill McCollum, a Florida congressman who was a leading force in the impeachment of President Bill Clinton.

"Nice to meet you," the congressman said to me. "I think Adam and I disagree on some issues, but he is one of the fairest reporters I've ever dealt with."

When a staunch Republican and a diehard Democrat agree a reporter is fair and balanced, that seems like an unequivocal ruling. Perhaps we need more testaments like this made public to restore confidence in the press.

logo illustration by Lee Burgess

— 9 —

No Dream Stealing

The third time I asked to speak to the owner of the Sara-sota boutique to see if she would like to stock the pock-etbooks I made out of books, her assistant gave me an un-clear response.

"I think she's all set," the young woman said.

"She's all set, like, she already has enough pocketbooks made out of books?" I asked.

"She's just all set," the assistant repeated in a chipper voice.

"Well after she got the samples, she emailed and said she loved them. Now I'm trying to figure out how many she wants to order," I explained.

"She just said to tell you she's all set," the assistant re-peated in the same cheerful, robotic tone.

Yet again, I hung up the phone without making my way into the retail market. I'd done well at holiday markets sell-ing more than 50 of the "book pocketbooks" made from hollowed out hardback copies of *Alice in Wonderland*, *To Kill a Mockingbird* and Nancy Drew's *Sign of the Twisted Candles*. I made the one-of-a-kind fashion *and* literary statements with books found at yard sales, a drill and a glue gun. But I was at a crossroads in my fashion career and needed to expand to retail stores.

The "business" started when my daughter Olivia, at age 9, unearthed a pink, plastic Hawaiian lei from the floorboard of my Honda Odyssey. She took the party favor from a past birthday and held it above a copy of Madonna's children's book *The English Roses*. Olivia turned the book sideways, holding the spine in her hand so the pages opened across the top.

"If we cut this lei in two and taped it to this book, it would be like handles to a pocketbook," said my little Thomas-Edison-meets-Coco-Chanel.

Within a week I had devised a way to make "Olivia's Book Pocketbooks." I still have a glue gun scar in the shape of Nevada on my left knee. The process called for an X-acto knife to slice pages out of the books' spines; a drill to make holes on the front and back covers; a hammer to secure little brass rings called grommets into each hole; a glue gun to attach accordion window shades along each side of the hollowed-out books; and ribbons to tie bamboo or tortoise-shell plastic handles to the newly created pocketbooks. Nothing to it.

In the beginning of the business venture, I woke Olivia early on Saturday mornings for yard sales, where we scouted for Nancy Drew classics, red-checkered Better Homes & Gardens cookbooks and coffee table books featuring artists such as Monet or Salvador Dali. After a month or so, Olivia gave me permission to do the shopping and assembling on my own, though she maintained creative control.

When Olivia's Book Pocketbooks debuted at a holiday bazaar in St. Petersburg, we made $400 profit after the cost of books, glue sticks and Band-Aids for my burns. I proudly took Olivia to a Bank of America branch to open an account. We ended up in the office of some 24-year-old male banker named Sid. I still remember the name because he was clueless, like the neighbor boy Sid who tried to execute Buzz Lightyear in *Toy Story*.

"This is Olivia's invention called Olivia's Book Pocketbooks. We are selling them for $35 to $50," I told Sid.

On cue, Olivia took the crumpled wad of 20s, 10s and 5s out of her yellow *Nancy Drew: Secret of the Old Clock* Book Pocketbook, which had matching yellow grosgrain ribbon handles.

Sid barely glanced at her or her product, making no effort to acknowledge or encourage the young entrepreneur.

"Okay. Will you be making automatic direct deposits of $300 or more on a monthly basis?"

"No. As I told you, this account is for a 9-year-old girl selling pocketbooks made out of old books. So, she doesn't have a routine direct deposit."

"Okay. Will she maintain a minimum daily balance of $2,000 or more?" Sid asked.

"That's unlikely for a while," I said. "We're just starting this little business."

"Okay, well then you're going to have to pay a monthly service fee," he said.

"No, she won't be paying a service fee each month," I said. "Because we are going to open an account at a bank where an employee with a pulse and a soul will have the decency to encourage a young businesswoman."

I thought back to my own custom dress business in the

late '80s and my first experience opening my own account at a bank.

I was 15, with a mere $250 in hand, but I was treated like Warren Buffet at what was then NCNB (Bank of America's predecessor) when I walked in with the first profits from sewing drop-waist jumpers that were Laura Ashley knockoffs.

My Aunt Carolyn, known for her careful business acumen, loaned me the seed money of $100 to buy checked and flowered flannel on sale at the Piece Goods Shop at what was then Raleigh's Cameron Village.

My dad, who adored Aunt Carolyn for her grit, resilience, humor and shrewd business mind was shocked. "I never thought Carolyn would loan a child $100. I bet she's charging you interest," he joked as she handed over the money.

Frugal as she was, Aunt Carolyn launched my first business. And when I had $250 cash collected in a plastic UNC cup on my dresser, my proud mother took me to open a bank account.

She had to co-sign on the account. As she completed the paperwork, she bragged on me just enough that soon five bankers and tellers were admiring the custom-made turquoise and black plaid jumper I just happened to be wearing. The branch manager ordered one just like it.

The enthusiasm from my mom, Aunt Carolyn, NCNB, and the high school and college friends who bought my dresses is still palpable decades later as I write this. That's probably why I was so annoyed by the Florida banker who offered no encouragement to Olivia, as well as the Sarasota boutique owner who was "all set."

They were dream stealers.

I'd never heard the term until my friend Elizabeth Whittely used it in a pep talk during those Book Pocketbook days. I had told her back then that my husband Adam jokingly said I made about 50 cents an hour for all the time I spent making and selling these creations Olivia pioneered.

"Uh-uh. No dream stealing," she said, waving her finger in the air. "Don't listen to any negativity."

Elizabeth was my best customer and muse, having bought five Book Pocketbooks for herself and friends, along with giving my name and number to more than 10 different people who admired her *To Kill a Mockingbird* Book Pocketbook on various business trips.

In my now-ex-husband's defense, he was cynical about the invention I kidnapped from our daughter, but it was all in humor. Adam brought our kids to visit my booth at all the places I hawked our goods, from synagogue courtyards to church basements to outdoor markets on downtown side streets.

And he managed to create a little levity after the horror of Hurricane Katrina at the expense of the Olivia's Book Pocketbook enterprise.

I registered on several websites offering to house New Orleans residents who needed a place to stay. The online surveys were long and detailed, perhaps in order to weed out bleeding hearts who wanted to help but weren't really equipped to host total strangers.

After filling out two pages of likes, dislikes, family structure, number of spare bedrooms, and daily living routines, I read the last question on one application aloud. "What attributes would help make a guest family acclimate to your household?"

"Handiness with a glue gun and drill," Adam said without missing a beat.

We were never matched with a family fleeing New Orleans, and the Book Pocketbooks never landed in a stylish boutique or major retail chain. There are dozens of handbags made out of books selling on Etsy now, but I'm proud Olivia's invention was the first one sold the year the online crafty marketplace debuted. She named her Etsy shop "The Chocolate Seashell" and uploaded all the images and information herself.

Then she moved on to middle school, and I gave up on going national.

Eventually I wrote a book instead of tearing one apart but revisited the Book Pocketbook endeavor when my friend Betsy helped host a book signing for me in Southern Pines. I wanted to give her a thank-you gift, but she owns a great boutique so what could I offer that she couldn't already get wholesale? Her shop, ETC., stood for Eloise Trading Company in honor of her favorite fictional character.

Ooooh la la. I got a "rawther" fabulous, fine, fine, fine idea and "skiddered" on over to JoAnn Fabrics for grommets and bamboo pocketbook handles. I made Betsy a Book Pocketbook from a hardback collection of four Eloise titles.

My middle daughter Charlotte was visiting from college and saw the telltale signs of a drill on the coffee table and rogue grommets spilled on the floor.

"What are you doing, Mom? Are you making Book Pocketbooks again?" she asked in the concerned tone someone might use when they find an empty gin bottle in the recycling bin of a recovered alcoholic.

I was self-employed and doing better than I expected with my own little PR firm, but when Charlotte smelled the combined scents of old books and hot glue, she worried I was back to my languishing fashion career.

"I made one for a friend as a special gift. I promise that's it. Just one," I assured her.

But I don't promise I won't try another long-shot venture at some point. Perhaps the vintage market is ripe for a comeback of those plaid flannel drop-waist dresses. There are plenty of reasons not to put your ideas out to the universe, such as dream-stealing store clerks and bankers. But there are many more enthusiastic friends, mothers, aunts and strangers to cheer them on.

— 10 —

Who Wore it Worse?

I walked past the plate glass window on Center Street five days in a row during our vacation on Nantucket to visit the tunic printed with pink and turquoise swirls. It was part '60s Twiggy and part '90s Trina Turk. It cost all parts of $150 and was out of my price range.

The year was 2004, my first time on Nantucket with my family and 16 years since I'd worked a summer on the island during college. Back then, I could have easily splurged on myself with the tips from one good night of waitressing in a waterfront restaurant, but by this time I was a mom of three and a low-paid newspaper reporter married to another low-paid newspaper reporter.

We used our tax refund to book a small cottage for a week in Nantucket, which held history for each of us. I lived and worked there with 11 friends in a three-bedroom house that summer in college. Adam, who hailed from New York City, grew up renting a house with his family every summer until he was about 15 years old.

So, with a joint love of the history-laden island covered in cobblestones and shingles, we took our family to Nantucket. This entailed flying from Tampa to Boston, taking a bus to Hyannis Port, a cab to the ferry, a ferry to Nantucket and finally landing in a two-bedroom cottage on Gardner Street.

The coffee table proudly offered up a photo album in which the owners shared the history of the 1800s house. The book included three pages documenting the 1999 construction of the bay window off the dining room that included a built-in bench seat with tufted cushions.

"Also known as the third bedroom," Adam said, because that's where 6-year-old Olivia slept while Charlotte, age 4, and Wade, age 2, shared a tiny room under the stairs.

But this story is not about that wonderful week of chilly days on Miacomet Beach or homemade ice cream at The Juice Bar. It's about fashion statements gone wrong.

Having found nothing I liked nearly as much, on our last day on the island, I bought that tunic right off the mannequin. I loved it. It was my go-to for special nights out, and I wore it in my column photo when I was the editor of a parenting magazine called *Go Momma*.

About six months after we returned from Nantucket, I heard my daughters yelling for me when I was upstairs giving Wade a bath. I wrapped him in a towel and rushed down the stairs to find them pointing to an episode of *Hannah Montana*.

There sat Vicki Lawrence portraying Hannah's grandmother while wearing my fabulous pink and turquoise tunic. Dolly Parton was playing the other, more youthful and fun grandmother and rocking a rhinestone bustier.

Are you kidding me? A Disney Channel costume

designer spotted my favorite shirt and decided it was perfect for Hannah's memaw? I was 33 years old at the time.

I don't mean to diminish Vicki Lawrence one bit. I love that hilarious redhead. I grew up adoring her and my other childhood idols on the *The Carol Burnett Show*. I just never thought I'd be up against her as a grandmother in *People* magazine's "Who Wore It Better?" column.

This wasn't my worst fashion offender though. The most regrettable wardrobe malfunction was the Wonder Woman costume I concocted for Halloween my freshman year in college.

It all started with a trip to a thrift shop. I dragged my friends there on October 29, hoping we'd find something that would beat their lame plan. It was our first Halloween in college, and they wanted to go as M&Ms. Each of us would wear all green, red, brown, yellow or blue and tape a lowercase "m" on our shirt.

When I found a vintage red, white and blue sequined leotard, I suggested we all go as a different superhero. Nobody felt the same urge to fight for justice, so I decided I'd save the world on my own.

"Katherine, I'm not saying you can't pull this off. But it's going to be cold and uncomfortable," my friend Beth advised.

"I'll sew a short, satin, flared skirt so I'm not just walking around in a sequined swimsuit all night," I said. The outfit was complete in my mind when I asked Carmen, a friend in my dorm, if I could borrow her white cowboy boots and she said yes. I bought golden electrical wire from the hardware store for the lasso and made bullet-repelling bracelets out of cardboard and aluminum foil.

At 7 p.m. on October 31, the flared skirt I'd sewed out of a white T-shirt instead of satin because I didn't have time to go to the fabric store made Wonder Woman look like she was wearing an adult diaper over her uniform. This is the moment Wonder Woman had her first beer of the night.

Around 7:30 p.m., Carmen made a last-minute costume switch to cowgirl and needed her white boots back. Wonder Woman went knocking on doors throughout Spencer Dorm looking to borrow another pair.

By 8 p.m., Wonder Woman had managed to scrounge up a pair of long white tube socks discarded by someone on the second floor who had decided not to dress up as a roller derby girl.

At 8:15 p.m., Wonder Woman put on some white Reeboks with the white tube socks and declared they looked almost, kind of, possibly like boots. Maybe? Wonder Woman opened another beer.

At 8:45 p.m., Wonder Woman, who looked like a discarded trapeze artist turned usher at some third-rate circus, really started second guessing her outfit.

"It's fine, Katherine. You look good. People will know you're Wonder Woman, or some kind of superhero. Or something," Beth said. "Besides. We're going to be at a packed party, nobody is going to be looking down at your tube socks."

"Or my diaper?" I asked.

"Or your diaper," she said. "You could still be an M&M."

"But I've already spent too much money on this stupid sequined thing."

At 8:50 p.m., Wonder Woman used her super strength to cut holes in the sides of two cans of Natural Light. She and a blue M&M turned those cans sideways, shotgunned their beers, then headed out into the cold night to meet up with the rest of the colorful candies.

At 9:30 p.m., while standing in a jam-packed Halloween party, Wonder Woman no longer worried people might notice her skirt looked like a diaper, her boots weren't boots and her lasso was just electrical wire. Nobody was looking at Wonder Woman, or the colorful candies, or even the cute cowgirls, the naughty nurses or the devilish devils.

Five girls wearing short black sleeveless dresses, 5-inch heels, heavy eye makeup and bright red lipstick with their hair pulled back in tight buns walked into the party single file. Somewhere in the room a clunky boombox played Robert Palmer's "Addicted to Love."

Conversations stopped. Jaws dropped. Drinks dropped. It's a good thing Wonder Woman was wearing that diaper.

The Robert Palmer Girls were in the house. Light years before twerking or soft porn were a given in music videos, the Robert Palmer Girls were about the sexiest thing going. In the late '80s, they were bold, beautiful, confident, sexy supermodels who didn't sing, twerk, or touch themselves. They barely even danced. There was some shoulder shifting and a slight sway of the hips here and there. But mostly they just looked bored and beautiful.

So, imagine the shock and awe when a slew of these sirens showed up at a college Halloween party. These girls commanded the room by performing minimal choreography and maximum pouting. When the performance ended, they were applauded like rock stars.

I wanted to shrink into the floor. Disappear. Evaporate. Even if I'd worn Carmen's boots and had Linda Carter's bustline, the Robert Palmer Girls were a thousand times more fabulous.

Over the next several days, there was camaraderie among the cute cowgirls and the vampy vampires, the foxy firefighters and the naughty nurses. Everybody felt like a zero compared to those Robert Palmer Girls.

Thirty years later, I brought up those Halloween Robert Palmer Girls to a group of friends from college who were reunited at a funeral for someone's father.

"Oh, I completely remember that. They were amazing," Hillary said.

"Everybody was staring at them. They were like 7 feet tall and gorgeous," Kelly added. "I felt like a little girl trick-or-treating compared to them."

"Who *were* those gorgeous girls?" Leigh asked.

We all laughed at the scene then, ourselves then, our insecurities then. Thirty years later we aren't immune to midlife second guessing, but women of a certain age have learned it's not the clothes that make or break us. Hannah and her memaw would probably agree.

— 11 —

By the Hair of My Chinny Chin Chin

In one episode of *Orange Is the New Black*, a character named Cindy is haunted by the same nemeses that haunt me. When she's being urged to run faster around the track, Cindy quips: "Man, I pluck my chin hairs, ain't that enough upkeep?"

I well remember the day two chin hairs first appeared in my life. It was that summer of '88 when I lived with friends on Nantucket Island. Twelve of us piled into a three-bedroom house that allowed only six occupants and worked at bistros, bike shops, ice cream spots and as chambermaids at historic inns.

Best. Summer. Ever.

Well, except for that day a group of us were watching a local summer league baseball game in the late afternoon, and the setting sun's light hit my chin at exactly the right angle.

"Oh my God! Katherine has hair growing out of her chin. There are two little black hairs growing out of her

Katherine Snow Smith

chin," Will, my friend since childhood, announced. He was sitting right next to me.

I used one hand to cover the evidence, and the other to smack him.

"Oh my God," he continued. "She's going to walk into Belk's with a full beard one day and say, 'Can I have some pantyhose, please?'" He said the last line in a low, guttural voice.

For many years, I have thought of that embarrassing but admittedly hilarious moment every time I have felt a blade of stubble on my chin. Whether it has been in the middle of a work meeting, a dark movie theater or sitting in church, the little hairs protruding an eighth of a millimeter have been fingernails on a chalkboard. For some reason, I have always blamed Will.

Since 1988, I have kept tweezers in every bathroom drawer, glove compartment and pocketbook to my name so I can be ready to pluck the two relentless imposters the second they emerge, usually four or five months after the last harvest.

Oddly, as my life has progressed from that carefree summer on Nantucket to motherhood, stressful jobs, health scares and all the other challenges of life, I have come to welcome those two little hairs. I now chuckle as I pluck the constants in my life and think of the exchange between Mrs. and Mr. Bennet in *Pride and Prejudice*.

"You take delight in vexing me. You have no compassion for my poor nerves," Mrs. Bennet complains to her husband when he throws up obstacles to her obsession with marrying off her daughters.

"You mistake me, my dear. I have a high respect for your nerves. They are my old friends," Mr. Bennet counters.

When my two old friends emerge every few months, they are reassuring in a strange way. Something that hasn't changed over all these years. They are a little problem that is quickly solved with my handy tweezers and magnifying mirror. Unlike most of life's issues, with chin hairs there's no wondering if I should have done this or tried that. No waiting it out. No sleepless nights. You notice them. You pluck them. You forget them. Repeat.

— 12 —

Sending Roses to My Husband's Girlfriend

My husband, our kids, my parents and I ate Thanksgiving lunch at the Cardinal Club in Raleigh in 2017. My parents enjoyed many flashbacks to the happy day they hosted our wedding reception at the top of the downtown Raleigh bank building in 1993. Twenty-four years later, nobody but Adam and I knew we were planning to end our marriage in a few months.

"So are we still going through with getting divorced?" Adam asked me as we took a walk through my parents' neighborhood after the gluttonous Thanksgiving meal.

"Yes we are," I said. I'm the one who called the time of death on our marriage after a year of weekly counseling following seven other marriage counselors over prior years. In the final session Adam said: "Sometimes we're fine. Sometimes it's pretty bad. I don't see that changing, but I feel like we can muddle through."

I was 49 at the time and not up for "muddling" for the rest of my life with no hope of things improving.

"Okay. Well then if we're really going through with this divorce, I'm going to start dating," Adam said as we walked along a street painted in autumn hues by the oak and maple leaves coating the ground.

He told me this right in front of the brick house on the hill at the corner of Rembert and Carteret Drives. This house gave out homemade popcorn balls on Halloween and was a highlight of trick-or-treating with my father and my longtime friend Elizabeth and her dad. I also waited in front of the same house to catch the bus to junior high. Sometimes my cousin Tripp would race by in his Jeep on his way to class at N.C. State and give me a ride to school. I felt so cool being dropped off in a Jeep instead of the bus.

The corner that held good memories for me became the place where my husband announced he'd be dating within a week. It was a hard moment. Granted, I had the painful luxury of deciding to get divorced. Spouses who are blindsided by a divorce have it much worse. But even when it's been a joint prospect for both husband and wife, it's still brutal because you're finally giving up on and letting go of the person you thought you loved more than anyone.

I was surprised Adam wouldn't wait until we were living separately, but I told him to go ahead.

About a week later, he and I were back in St. Petersburg a few blocks from our house walking our dog along the shore of Tampa Bay.

For 20 years we'd spent our morning walks with one, two or three children in strollers and our dogs—first with an ornery basset hound named Delbert and then with an overly eager-to-please mutt named Charlie. Between picking up books and pacifiers dropped from the stroller, we'd talk about what stories we were working on. At first, we were both reporters, but at this point he was the newspaper's political editor, and I was editor of the arts and culture magazine called *Bay*.

"So I'm covering this vintage holiday market Friday for *Bay*," I told him.

"I have a date Friday," he said flatly.

And now we were in some new territory.

"Anybody I know?" I asked.

"No, I just went on Match.com."

"Where are you going?" I asked.

"Well, remember you were telling me about the story you're doing on that new upscale food place in the old warehouse in Tampa? I got a reservation there," he said.

"Glad I could help you out," I said with no emotion and walked ahead of him.

Once again, a painful new reality intersected with a former Shangri-la. We were walking through the palm arboretum along Tampa Bay. I used to stroll Olivia and Charlotte to this winding brick path shaded by more than a dozen varieties of palms to meet Adam for lunch once a week. He'd bring takeout from a sandwich shop downtown and thrill the girls with a midday game of hide-and-seek.

And now, in the same special place, we were living the final days of our marriage.

I could have left the house early that Friday night to avoid awkwardness, but I felt like he shouldn't get off that easy.

I don't think I've been just sitting on the sofa doing nothing but reading a magazine on a Friday night since the kids were born. But on this particular night, I calmly flipped through the pages of the most recent *Vanity Fair*. Adam had to go right past me to get out the front door.

He walked by with no eye contact and no comment.

"Have funnnn," I bellowed in a cheerful tone akin to Marion Cunningham sending Richie off to the prom.

I got home from the vintage holiday decor market around 9 p.m. and went straight to the guest room. I put in earphones and started streaming a movie, so I didn't have to hear Adam come in or know what time he came in.

The next morning as I headed out the door to exercise, Adam was eating breakfast.

"How was the vintage market thing?" he asked.

"It was good. I got a 1950s pitcher shaped like Santa and some brass deer candle holders," I answered. "How was your date?"

"It was good. I mostly did it to piss you off, but I like her. We're going out again."

We didn't make any more small talk or have any big arguments about his dating that day because we had to prepare dinner for 12 people. It was our once-a-year turn to host supper club.

After making shrimp and grits, crab cakes, rosemary biscuits and green beans, we set the table at the last minute. I filled the new, old Santa pitcher with ice water while he placed the gorgeous bone-china plates that had been his great-grandmother's around the table.

As everyone served themselves from the buffet, a guest somehow dropped one of the antique plates. Adam's face went stark white, then red, as he turned visibly blue. Later the wife of the plate-breaker apologized profusely to me in the kitchen saying she could tell Adam was pretty irked.

"Believe me, I couldn't care less," I said. "We're getting divorced, but we aren't telling anyone until after

Christmas. Adam has already gone on Match.com and started dating."

"You gotta be kidding me. Want me to break the rest of his plates? Or maybe his kneecaps?" she said. It made me laugh, and we both shook our heads and rolled our eyes. What are you gonna do?

Adam and I decided to still use tickets we'd bought a few months earlier to see Jim Gaffigan on New Year's Eve in Tampa. After all, many things hadn't changed or been erased. We shared a similar sense of humor and both liked the comedian who honestly addressed raising kids, marriage and growing older. I didn't think twice when Adam was texting a few times during the show; he was always working on a story. Then I did wonder, who from the political realm was texting with him at 10 p.m. on New Year's Eve? I glanced over at his phone and saw he was texting with the girl he'd been dating. What would Jim Gaffigan do with that?

The day we told our children was truly one of the worst days of my life, and thinking back on it still makes me feel sick. Adam and I had worked out a settlement with little friction and no need to go to court. We maintained one joint credit card for family expenses and would split the bill down the middle after the house sold.

I opened the Visa bill in early March and quickly glanced at the past month's charges.

"Oh, hell no," I said aloud, staring at the $65 charge for 1-800-Flowers on February 14. I called my soon-to-be-ex-husband.

"So did your girlfriend like the roses we sent her for Valentine's?"

"What are you talking about?"

"You charged the flowers you sent her on our joint credit card."

"Oops. I'll pay all of that," he said.

"Yeah. That goes without saying."

An older friend of mine who divorced when her kids were in college told me that she and her husband said some pretty rough things to each other when they were going through the process. Neither was acting like their true self. But the bad behavior on both sides didn't last, and she and her ex went on to be close friends. I'm glad to say that's how Adam and I are.

Still, I'd never make it on *The Bachelorette*. It was hard enough living with him while he was dating. I think it would be even harder living with the woman or women he was romancing.

But at least on *The Bachelorette*, ABC pays for the roses.

— 13 —

Watch as I Dive In

Six months into the COVID-19 pandemic, I started swimming several days a week at the nearby public pool. New safety measures dictating one person in every other lane made swimming much less stressful than when I hit the pool for laps before work in years past. Before COVID, we had as many as four people in a lane, and on several occasions, I accidentally grazed the bare ribcage of my boss, the newspaper's publisher, who also swam laps.

My friend Caroline alerted me to the pool's one-swimmer-per-lane status when I lamented that I was waking up at 5 a.m. in order to take a brisk walk before the temperature hit 95 and it became necessary to constantly wipe the sweat dripping from my mask.

"When I try to run these days, my body is like: 'Who the hell do you think you are? You are too old for this,'" Caroline told me. "Swimming is easy on the body but also the ultimate cross training. You totally disconnect. It's how I've kept my sanity during COVID."

She was right.

In my own lane, under water, I felt completely free of all the chaos, confusion and heartache of COVID. No iP-hones underwater. No newscasts. No traumatic grocery store runs. Not even a podcast about self-improvement or unsolved mysteries.

How ironic that swimming would bring me peace in my 50s, when it was the albatross around my neck as a teenager.

At age 13, I arrived at beloved Camp Seafarer on the NC coast barely knowing how to swim a proper stroke. My parents had taken me to swim class as a young child, and I'd spent thousands of happy hours in the pool and in the Atlantic Ocean, but when asked to put in eight laps for the required swim test on the second day of camp, I looked more like I was hanging wallpaper than swimming.

My fellow cabinmates, as well as almost every camper above the age of 7, easily passed the swim test and wore a white band around their neck to prove it. I was saddled with a black band so counselors could easily identify me as a drowning risk, as well as someone who couldn't check out a boat without a counselor on board, go down the giant waterslide, or jump from a platform onto the enormous inflated yellow-and-red "Blob" that bounced you high into the air before your landing in the lake.

The only level lower was "red band" status, which was designated for girls who started swallowing water as fast as they could upon entering the pool and had no concept of staying in the shallow end. There were a couple red bands in Cabins 1 and 2, and a few black bands in Cabins 3 to 10.

But when Cabins 11 through 40 stood up in the mess hall and declared themselves "100 percent White Band,"

Cabin 28 quietly sucked our Pudding Pops because of the black elastic band hanging around my neck. My albatross.

While my cabin mates took diving and water ballet during daily instructional swim each morning, I was in a basic strokes class with a girl from Japan who spoke no English and a girl with developmental delays.

We were taught the sidestroke by an encouraging counselor with a southern drawl who made it as fun as possible.

"So today, y'all, we are on a farm and we're pickin' cherries. You reach down with your left arm for your bucket and at the same time reach up with your right to grab some bright, red, shiny cherries off the tree," she explained as she stood on the wooden dock showing us the motions. "You bring your bucket up to your waist and your cherries down to your bucket at the same time with your hands cupped. Then you push one arm down for the next bucket and the other arm back up to the tree."

Of course, our legs were scissor-kicking, which we had practiced for two days on kickboards before advancing to the arm choreography.

I recently found a letter my father sent at the time. "Katherine, try not to worry about the swimming levels. Work at it, and you will get better. But more importantly, remember you are a person in your own right."

At age 13, I'm sure his words buoyed me. In my 50s, I looked up the exact meaning of "person in their own right." The phrase means a person is successful or respected because of their own efforts and talents rather than those of the people they are closely connected with. Good words of support for anyone at any age.

I remember facing my cabinmates during the nightly devotional circle and telling them I was sorry I was holding back our group's 100 percent at such a basic accomplishment. I told them I was picking my cherries best I could and got them laughing by demonstrating the bucket-to-waist, cherries-to-bucket maneuvers.

Two weeks into the four-week session, when I retested for a white band, all of Cabin 28 assembled on grass beside the swim lake yelling in unison: "Hey Katherine, pick your cherries! We love you!"

It was just like the scene from *An Officer and a Gentleman* when Richard Gere has some kind of detention doing extra hours of training with Lou Gossett Jr. on a mountain by the water. His love interest Debra Winger and another couple zoom by in a boat and moon him to show their support.

Ceil Baldwin, the counselor overseeing the Seafarer swim lake, certainly wasn't as tough as Lou Gossett Jr., but I think she was just as proud of me when I earned that white band as he was when Gere's character Mayo, whom he called Mayonnaise, graduated from Navy Aviation Officer Training.

When I retested, I completed the required number of various strokes with better form and no signs of taking on water. Ceil was waiting on the lake's dock when I emerged and ceremoniously removed my black band to replace it with a white band.

This was a defining moment of my childhood. I overcame a deficit by openly admitting my embarrassment and working hard. Friends and counselors supported me.

Decades later when my daughters were campers at Seafarer, I learned girls were tying knots in the middle of their swim bands to signify if they had a boyfriend at Camp Sea Gull, the brother camp up the river. Geeze. It was a whole new kind of swim band pressure beyond proficient strokes.

I didn't worry much about correct form during my mid-COVID aquatic workouts in St. Petersburg. My goal was simply to get from one side of the pool to the other. But my swimming insecurities resurfaced when I noticed the front desk clerk usually assigned me to the first or second lane right below the lifeguard stand.

Were my flailing strokes as much of a telltale sign of my inadequacies as the black band? More than once I thought I caught the lifeguards exchanging knowing smiles as one took over the other's post.

"Yep. Now it's your turn to watch her," they seemed to commiserate.

As much as I tell myself and my kids that age brings an increased immunity to caring what others think, some traces of our insecurities will always linger like the smell of chlorine in your hair.

— 14 —

I'll Never Meet Sven
at Flyleaf Books

hile I was finding my footing back in North Carolina, I decided to make this next chapter of my life even more complicated by trying online dating again. Three years had passed since I dipped my toe into St. Petersburg's Bumble six months after my divorce was final. I never even made it out of the house and deleted the app after two weeks of pointless messaging.

I thought the online dating pool in Raleigh and Chapel Hill might offer more options.

I cringed when I finished writing my profile but closed my eyes and posted it. I cringed more reading the profiles of potential suitors. Men were either sharing too much about their innermost feelings or showing endless photos of their workout routine. They wanted to meet "a soulmate with whom I can slow down and smell the roses" or "a woman who can keep up with someone who runs an average of 40 miles a week and benches 225 pounds."

I gravitated toward the men who didn't feel the need to expose their life story or post a lengthy list of likes and dislikes. I steered clear of the ones who posted nothing but photos. Looks count, but so do a sense of humor, a job, outside interests and the ability to write a complete sentence without confusing your and you're.

Of course, it didn't matter what criteria I used because it felt just as unsuccessful as Bumble in St. Petersburg. The few men I liked didn't like me back, and the ones who liked me were far from my type.

My profile stated I was a 50-something journalist with a college degree. Still, 70-year-old men standing shirtless flying a Confederate flag were eager to meet and see where the night took us.

"I don't get it. People meet all the time on these things," my friend Beth said after I'd been on Match.com for two weeks and not encountered one potential date.

"I know. I swear I'm not being overly picky," I replied. "I know I'm light years away from Jennifer Anniston or Nicole Kidman, but I think I look okay for a middle-aged woman in Raleigh, North Carolina."

"Did you put anything about your book on there? And the good reviews?" she asked.

"No. I thought that would look like bragging."

I explained that you can either just "wink" at someone's profile or wink and also send a message.

"You should set a goal of finding six good prospects and writing a message to each," she suggested.

I concocted what I thought were clever individualized messages to the public policy teacher at UNC who was a big fan of author David Sedaris, the civil engineer who posted photos of his compost bin and the investment banker who loved being a girl dad.

I needed three more and scrolled through the app with Beth.

We cringed at the shirtless man riding a horse on the beach and choked on our wine at the man in the Speedo with long white hair and the body of a young Arnold Schwarzenegger.

"This insurance guy from Burlington looks nice. He only posted two photos," Beth said, pausing at one profile. I gave him a wink and messaged that I liked the fact that he posted just two photos.

"What about him?" Beth asked, handing me my phone with a photo of a nice-looking man about my age who was a physical therapist.

"His profile only states his job and that he loves Carolina basketball and his dog. Not a lot to go on," I said.

"Well, you love Carolina basketball and your dog. You already have two things in common."

I gave the physical therapist a wink and asked his dog's name and what he thought of this year's team.

One more to go.

"What about this guy?" Beth asked.

"His hair is so spiky. He's got more gel in that photo than I've ever used in my whole life."

"I know it's not what you're used to. But read his profile."

Sven was from Switzerland. He moved to Chapel Hill to teach and was feeling out of place but eager to meet locals and find a good independent bookstore.

"Hello Sven," I messaged. "I grew up a whole 30 miles down the road in Raleigh, and I'm feeling a bit out of place myself. Flyleaf Books is a great local bookstore."

The next day only one potential suitor had winked back at me.

"What about the guy with the dog?" Beth asked.

"No response."

"You're way out of his league anyway. What about Sven?"

"Nada."

"*Sven* didn't reply? What is *Sven's* deal?" Beth demanded incredulously.

It's tough out there. At least the insurance guy from Burlington seemed funny. He responded to my comment about only posting two photos with: "I'm bald and depressed in all my other pictures."

We texted a bit and made plans to meet in Chapel Hill for a drink.

The day before our rendezvous he messaged me: "What are you looking for?"

Uggggh. I barely knew this guy. I'm a pretty open person, but I cringed at this invasive question.

I was talking to my friend Molly in St. Petersburg when I got the text.

"Tell him you're looking for someone who doesn't ask a stupid question like that," she said.

We deduced he was trying to find out if I was interested in a one-night stand or a walk down the aisle. I wanted neither.

"I'm new to online dating. Not used to this question," I messaged. "What are you looking for?"

"Good company. Someone to go to concerts with. Someone to travel with," he replied.

It wasn't a lot to ask in theory. But how could he even consider a second date, much less a vacation, without meeting me in person? By no means did I think he was so taken with my photos and profile that he was ready to head to Paris. His question was probably typical of strangers navigating dating in the later phases of life. But I was more used to these topics coming up organically over time. I opted for a meaningless response: "I'll bring my passport."

"Pack lightly," he responded. I smiled.

We met at 411 West, an Italian restaurant on Chapel Hill's main drag, and sat at the bar. He quickly disparaged the selection of North Carolina craft beers. I admitted I wasn't adventurous or sophisticated enough to embrace the craft beer movement and still preferred a Miller Light.

"That's like still watching cable when you can stream a thousand shows," my date said.

"Well, full disclosure, I do stream new shows, but I still love catching *The Andy Griffith Show* on TV Land."

He asked if I loved North Carolina so much, why wouldn't I choose to support a local brewery instead of a huge conglomerate. Points for challenging me.

"You're right. I need to find a North Carolina beer I like," I said. "I do love wine from Shelton Vineyards out of Surry County. My dad is from there, and we go to the vineyard about every year."

"If you're going to support a North Carolina wine, that's about the worst one in the state," he huffed.

It's one thing to be challenging, but another to be downright rude. Then I had the worst insecure dating thought. Was this guy sabotaging himself because he didn't like me and wanted to end the date ASAP? Was he chewing off his leg to free himself from the trap of sitting at a bar with me?

He ordered another Olde Hickory Piedmont Pilsner and told me he'd been married twice, each time for less than three years, "because she was batshit crazy."

I guessed he was keeping all limbs intact.

"I got divorced after 24 years. I was perfect. It was all his fault," I offered up with a sly smile.

"That's what all women think," he replied, clueless to my sarcasm.

We talked about our work. Our favorite movies. He had no kids and didn't really like kids. I told him I had three, but didn't like kids either.

He smiled slightly.

I was wondering if two drinks constituted a date and was weighing my exit strategies when the man to my right asked if he could glance at my menu. He was wearing a red leather jacket with the words "Liquid Pleasure" on the back.

Those two words unearthed momentous nights in college, as well as a few friends' weddings. I also remembered my former husband asking me the day after Barack Obama was first elected: "Have you ever heard of Liquid Pleasure from Chapel Hill? They are playing with James Taylor for the inauguration."

Well, of course I'd heard of Liquid Pleasure. The Chapel Hill-born band was legendary and known for fabulous dance music and a great rapport with its audiences.

I asked the man in the leather jacket if he was with the band and learned he was the founder and front man, Kenny Mann.

I cited my gig as a freelance reporter for *Business North Carolina* magazine and started asking how they kept the band going for so long. Early on, Kenny had realized the perfect business plan. The college parties Liquid Pleasure played for in the '80s and '90s were loss leaders. A few years after they graduated, the band played at their weddings and business events for five times what they charged for a college function. Now they play 150 shows a year, mostly weddings. They are booked across the country and do nuptials in Mexico and Italy too.

I introduced myself and my date to Kenny, then kept asking questions and typing notes on my phone.

Liquid Pleasure started out as four cousins in middle school. Dean Smith's oldest daughter played the clarinet with them briefly. Kenny's father was the chef at the Rathskeller and invented that lasagna with the cheese stretching table-to-mouth.

Even with their motto "the more you drink the better we sound," nobody in the band drinks or smokes. And guess how Liquid Pleasure got on Barack Obama's radar when he made a campaign stop at the Dean Dome?

"When we used to play at Princeton, I met a girl named Michelle Robinson from Chicago. She was running around with Brooke Shields," Kenny told us. Well, it was more like Kenny told only me. By this time my date was staring forward, not engaging in the conversation.

I guess I was rude. If he had started leaning hard to the other side of his barstool to talk to someone else, maybe I'd be annoyed. But not if she or he was a really interesting person.

Clearly, neither of us was overly interested in the other. I suggested we get the check, and he asked if it was okay to split it down the middle. I quickly agreed, even though my frugal mind was calculating how much more his craft beer cost than my lowbrow domestic.

We walked outside 411 West and started to bid our goodbyes.

"How do you think this went?" he asked, catching me way off guard. I was new to this immediate feedback portion of a first date, which is apparently status quo with on-line dating.

The antiquated old-school side of me was annoyed with how much things have changed. I feel the same way when a stranger asks me to take a photo with their phone then won't let me leave until it's deemed fabulous with all eyes open and smiles perfect. I remember a simpler time. When someone asked you to take a picture of their family in front of Cinderella's castle at Disney World, you pointed, clicked and moved on to Fantasyland without having to wait for a critique.

So there my Match.com date and I stood on Franklin Street, with him waiting on a live review. I panicked for a minute then thought about how my humor fell flat. He was disappointed in my choice in beer and conversation with barmates. He didn't seem taken with me, so why should I feel badly about not being taken with him? Still, it was awkward to call a spade a spade.

"I enjoyed meeting you, and this was fun. If you want to catch a daytime art festival or have lunch sometime, that would be nice."

"Have a nice life," he countered and walked away.

Uggh. I can tell myself I was nice and diplomatic, but I wasn't. Nobody is on Match.com to find a lunch date. It would have been better to just say I didn't think we were a good match. I doubt he was really crushed. He probably had three other dates that week.

Still, I decided that was my last attempt at online dating. Thousands of very nice, wonderful people meet online every day without being unkind or fake. I just can't take the rejection and rejecting others long enough to get the hang of it.

I'll stick to Fantasyland and leave a shoe behind next time I go to 411 West, or perhaps just write my phone number on the bathroom wall.

— 15 —

The Dating Game

As much as that statistic saying 50 percent of marriages end in divorce is bandied about, nowhere near half the people I know are divorced. Thus, the pool of folks, especially men around my age, who are single is smaller than that suspiciously yellow "baby pool" next to the "big pool" I frequented as a child and again when I was raising my own children.

If you aren't on dating apps fishing in waters stocked with single people who are somewhat interested in meeting someone, the odds of going out on a date are low. The odds of going out on a great date: even lower.

"I finally decided to just go out with anyone who asked me, even if I knew it wasn't going to be a great date," my friend Hale, who didn't marry until her late 30s, told me recently. "So when this guy who was friends with someone a friend of mine was dating asked me out, I just agreed.

"He shows up at my door with a box of Whitman's chocolates. It was nice, but seemed like something you'd see on *The Waltons*. Then he asked me if I felt claustrophobic living in my little condo, which I'd just bought all on my own."

Maybe the chocolates were supposed to soften the blow of his attack on her pride and joy.

"I so wanted to pretend I suddenly had food poisoning, but that would have been really mean," she said. "We got in his car, and he asked if I was okay with bar food instead of a restaurant. I was more than fine with that because I wanted a stiff drink and thought the date would end faster. So he took me to this bar—and I'm not making this up—where they were having an erotic poetry reading."

She had one drink and took a cab home. Alone, needless to say.

Another friend, who is in her early 70s but looks like she's early-60-something, laughingly reeled off several bad dates.

"I met one man for lunch, and I don't think he asked me a single question until the bill arrived and he said, 'We're splitting this, right?' I had ordered a salad, and he got a steak and a martini," she recounted. "I put down my credit card and said I would cover both of us. I didn't want him to think he was doing me any favors."

On her next blind date, she left the table before the check arrived. In fact, she left the table before the food arrived. Her date showed up with another woman.

"At first I thought maybe it was his sister or a friend who drove him there," she recounted. "Then they made it clear they were looking for a threesome."

Now, in a way, she beat the odds. What are the odds of that after age 70?

Other than dating a former college crush for a while

and the one-and-done Match.com date, I've been set up on a couple blind dates and even met someone by texting the wrong number.

The first blind date evolved after running into my friend Allison, who I hadn't seen in 20 years or so. She said she's something of a matchmaker and would think of someone to fix me up with. In less than an hour she decided on a man she knows who she said is funny, a Democrat and a fan of live music.

I had thought back to one of my very first live shows when I walked past UNC's Memorial Hall the next day. I saw R.E.M. there in the late '80s. What I remember most about the concert is Michael Stipe's comment, which appeared the next day at the bottom of the front page of *The Daily Tar Heel* as the quote of the day. Between songs, someone in the audience dared to yell out "Superman," the band's big hit from 1986.

"We don't take requests. Besides, I hate that song," Stipe quipped.

Need the *DTH* or I say more?

Back to me as an adult with the prospect of a blind date with the music fan. I told Allison I actually loved one song by this random group called Shakey Graves and they were playing in Raleigh the next week. I'd asked a few friends to go, but nobody was available. So the matchmaker introduced us on a text saying something like:

"I told Katherine you like live music and she's a big fan of this band called Broken Coffins or Wavey Graves or something like that. It's playing here next week."

Within a few days he'd found out Shakey Graves was actually not a band but a solo performer named Alejandro Rose-Garcia and bought tickets.

"He was also in *Spy Kids 3*. You vouch for this guy?" he asked in a text.

"Not at all," I replied. "I only know one song, 'Dearly Departed.'"

"Why do you like it?" he asked.

"It's actually weird because I'm way into song lyrics and what they mean, but I can't figure this one out. It's a man and a woman singing about how they both know that the house is haunted. She's looking for her crystal ball, and he's busy trying to charm that snake. Let me know your analysis."

He texted a few days later.

"So I think they are moving on from each other and trying to ignore their lingering feelings, which haunt them. And he's got ED."

"Okay. Makes sense. But I don't get the part about education?" I asked.

"Not education," he responded. "Erectile dysfunction."

Yes. I unknowingly made chitchat about erectile dysfunction with a total stranger and future date.

By the time I was on my way to the restaurant to meet my date before going to see the former child star sing about his troubles in the boudoir, I was regretting the whole setup. My discomfort wasn't really nerves, but probably because of my same aversion to online dating. I just like knowing someone before going out with him.

I arrived first and was seated at a big, very big, square table in the middle of a loud, very loud, restaurant. The place settings were way across from each other, and I pictured myself constantly asking him to repeat himself.

I moved his place setting to my right, then looked around and saw that at every other table with just two people they were sitting across from each other. I moved the placemat and silverware back across the table just as he approached.

"I won't be able to hear you all the way over there," he said, as he moved the well-traveled placemat and silverware back beside me.

Conversation flowed easily, and by the time the bill arrived, we were teasing each other about some of the personal shortcomings we'd divulged and discussing education versus erectile dysfunction.

Two days later, we went out again. He kissed me on the lips in public when he saw me, and when the waitress commented how deep in conversation we were, he joked that we were celebrating our five-year anniversary. He'd started reading my first book and loved it, but said he preferred to hear each story in person. He told me he was struck by my dark eyes gleaming across the restaurant when he walked in for the first date.

"Okay. So full confession," I admitted. "I moved the placemat and silverware next to me before you got there that night because they were so far apart. Then I moved it back across the table because nobody else was right next to each other, and I was worried you might notice."

"And I moved it back next to you," he said. "It's fate."

Guess what? When somebody says it's fate, it's not. That's only in Hallmark movies.

A week or so later he mentioned his office holiday party, and I asked if he was taking someone else since he didn't ask me.

That was a mistake. I realized later that even with our comfort level and his romantic remarks, it was way too early to be thinking I was a plus-one for a work event.

He used words like "reset" and "right size" when he canceled our next date in a text.

It hurt. A lot. But I took it well and promised he wouldn't find any rabbits boiling on his stove. We're friends now.

I'd pled ignorance and an aversion to playing games to my married girlfriends when I told them I asked about the office party and freaked him out.

"I'm still new at all this. I'm used to saying whatever I'm thinking after 24 years of marriage," I explained.

They agreed dating is confusing but concluded it's still a game of cat and mouse.

"And next time, just run what you're gonna say past one of us before you text it," said one married friend who hasn't had to navigate dating since *Cheers* was on the air.

I appreciate my married friends' tips from the sidelines, but they don't really know what it's like to be in the game these days with fewer prospects who are carrying more baggage and the invention of the cell phone and social media.

Back when they were single and I was in my first round of dating, we tried to decipher what someone was thinking via answering machine messages, or a lack of messages. At some point the high-tech "*69" came into play. Dialing that on a push-button landline allowed you to see who the most recent caller was, even if he or she didn't leave a message.

Nine times out of ten, it was your mom, not that crush who you hoped was just too nervous to leave a message.

When email entered the dating game, I was married and thankfully on my 24-year dating hiatus, but Tom Hanks and Meg Ryan educated me in *You've Got Mail*.

Now, texts are the tea leaves one must dissect and disseminate. Even I know not to send two texts in a row without hearing from the other side of the court. (This dating suicide is known as "double texting.") And when the competitor tosses up a friendly serve, you don't return it within the same hour or perhaps the same day. A steady volley may occur, but don't let it be the norm early on.

I went out with one man who texted me several times a day after our first date. I enjoyed him more in person than on the phone.

"How's your day going so far?" he texted at 9:30 a.m.

I replied with a thumbs-up emoji.

"I'm swamped at work," he texted after lunch. I didn't reply, because, well, he was swamped, right? Also, I wanted to hint that I wasn't into texting if there was nothing to say.

When we saw each other in person again, he was fun and challenging, but something was a little off.

The next week he sent more pointless texts naming multiple people I didn't know. Ultimately, I realized he liked to check in with me frequently, but really wanted to talk more about himself, via text as well as in person.

I told him over the phone—during a call, not a text—that our few dates had been fun, but we just seemed to be interested in different things.

Perhaps the most complicated dating terrain is social media. It offers countless ways to tell if someone has liked or ignored you, opened a story, commented on the story or posted photos with or without you. I was never a regular on Facebook and left Instagram much to the distress of my 2.3 million* followers more than two years ago. (*A slight exaggeration.)

It may hurt Team Katherine to not use social media to my advantage, but I think throwing in the white towel serves me better than trying to master it.

Along with new communication lines in dating, the basic game pieces don't mean what they used to. I had no idea until I was divorced how many married men don't wear wedding rings.

The phrase "wheels up, rings off," has been used in many books and articles to describe a culture among reporters, politicians and, more recently, Secret Service agents who abandon their marital status once the plane takes off.

The misplaced wedding band is also common in country songs.

In Miranda Lambert's "Ugly Lights" she refers to bars full of people with wedding rings hidden in pockets.

In "Am I Right or Amarillo," Jack Ingram admits to a potential paramour that he's put his ring on a keychain and her diamond is in her pocketbook. Of course, I knew rings were removed for nefarious reasons. But I had no idea until I was divorced how many happily married people, mostly men, with no aspirations of cheating don't wear rings.

About a year after I was divorced, I settled into the middle seat on a Southwest flight from Raleigh to Tampa and put up my usual invisible forcefield. Earphones in ears. Book in lap. No eye contact with passengers on either side.

As soon as the plane reached whatever altitude allowed laptops, I began working on whatever story was due the next morning. On this Sunday afternoon, the man to my left leaned over to retrieve the notebook my Diet Coke nudged off the tray table.

"Isn't this a reporter's notebook?" he asked, handing me the long, narrow pad.

"Good eye. Yes, it is," I said, as I noticed he wasn't wearing a wedding ring.

He asked if I was a journalist and told me he was an obstetrician. We talked for twenty minutes until he mentioned his wife, and the pieces suddenly came together.

Obstetricians don't wear wedding rings because their hands need to be bare and immaculate to bring life into the world.

Here's who else may opt to go sans wedding rings: golfers, sailors, tennis players, porn stars, hand models and at least one man who broke his ring using it to open a bottle of beer. (His wife was not pleased.)

Allison, the matchmaker, told me her husband quit wearing his band after she squeezed his hand so hard during labor that some blood vessels broke.

Married celebrities who reportedly have kept their left hand bare at times include Prince William, Beyoncé, Jay-Z, Ivanka Trump, Donald Trump, Will Smith, Jada Pinkett Smith, Viola Davis, Meredith Vieira and former UK Prime Minister David Cameron.

Let's get back to the mortals.

A few years ago, my ex-husband and I took our son to an out-of-state college where he'd been accepted. After a good tour and fun dinner, they retired to their room to watch a movie. I went to the hotel bar for a glass of wine and started talking with a half dozen other parents of prospective students. The conversation splintered into a one-on-one chat with a man who said his daughter was deciding between the school we were visiting, which was his alma mater, and Colgate University, "where my daughter's mother went."

Translation: when someone without a wedding ring says "daughter's mother" instead of "my wife," he's divorced. Or so I thought.

As the hotel bar announced last call, an alumna in the group who grabbed my hand like I was her freshman roommate, though we'd just met, insisted everyone go to a local dive two blocks away.

I didn't argue with my new bestie or the DC lobbyist, a Harrison Ford look-alike, who bought me a drink for the road. The bar was packed with students harboring fake IDs and a good dose of alums who hadn't been carded in decades. My newfound freshman roomie knew the bartender and got him to play the late '80s setlist on her phone.

Harrison Ford and I danced until sweat poured.

"This is so much fun. My wife hates to dance," he said when we took a break.

"You're married?" I asked when our faces were about 5 inches apart and he'd bought me another drink.

"Yeah, 26 years," he replied.

"Are you kidding me? Why aren't you wearing a wedding ring?" I asked.

"I just don't. My father-in-law never wore one either."

"Is that so? Well, I didn't know your father-in-law didn't wear his wedding ring because I didn't know you had a father-in-law, or a wife. You never mentioned any of that."

"Sure I did. I'm not trying to do anything wrong here," he said.

"No, you only mentioned her as your 'daughter's mother.' Why are you buying me drinks and dancing if you're married?" I asked.

"Because you are fun and interesting. That's all," he replied. "No harm, no foul."

I walked my fun and interesting self right out of that bar and called a bigtime foul. The *real* Harrison Ford would never do that.

Considering the changing rules and dismal odds, it was like winning a scratch-off lottery when I texted a wrong number and struck up an exchange with a divorced man who was a sarcastic, smart scientist and had actually read my first book at his aunt's beach house near Charleston.

The accidental meeting started when I ran into an old friend with the nickname of "Teamo" at a UNC football game and promised to send his wife my book.

"Hey. It's Katherine Snow Smith. Good seeing you yesterday," I texted the next morning. "Send me your address, and I'll mail you a book for your wife."

"This is some pretty sophisticated artificial intelligence using a local author. I've actually read her book and it's good," he replied.

I showed it to my friend Hilburn, who lived in Teamo's hometown. Neither of us got his humor.

"Actually, Hilburn can bring you the book since y'all live near each other in Greensboro. Just tell me exactly how to spell your wife's name so I can sign it."

"Delilah," he replied.

"What's he talking about? Her name is Sue Ellen. I just can't remember if there's a hyphen or not," Hilburn said.

"Ha ha," I texted, hinting that his joke wasn't so funny. "Hilburn doesn't know if there's a hyphen or not."

"Now the AI is using one of the most unusual names I've ever heard. She's a real estate agent here. Pretty impressive. Stop texting me," he replied.

Hilburn and I looked at each other with confused faces.

"What is he talking about?" she asked.

"Teamo used to be really funny. What's going on?" I said.

"I don't think this is Teamo," she said. "Maybe you put the wrong number in your phone."

Hilburn solved the mystery.

"This is not a scam. I really am Katherine Snow Smith. I'm trying to text a friend in Greensboro to sign a book for his wife. Maybe I have the wrong number," I texted.

After some "who's on first, what's on second," we realized several things: I had a wrong number; a friend of his knew Hilburn; we were both divorced and about the same age; and we had a lot in common.

"When I read your book, I thought we had the same sense of humor," he texted. "We owe it to the kismet gods to meet."

We made plans for dinner in Chapel Hill the next weekend.

"Let me ask you this. Are you really planning to go out with a man you met from a wrong number?" one of my married friends said when I told her of the crazy chance encounter.

"Yes, I am. I'm meeting him in a public place and can leave anytime I want," I said. "I've been telling you it's hard to meet single men, and this one fell into my lap."

The first date with Mr. Wrong Number was good. Not great, but good. He was interesting, smart and good-looking.

I felt no spark, but that doesn't always come at first. We went out a week later.

On the second date I found myself looking for a reason to rule him out.

"I don't watch TV except for sports," he said.

Well, that's it, I thought. He's too highbrow, looking down on the masses who are loving this latest golden age of television.

"Well good for you for not wasting your time," I said nicely. "But aren't you a little curious about *Ozark* or *Dopesick*?"

"Those are two of my favorites. I stream all the time," he explained.

Okay, only a few points off for his overly exact distinction between "watching" and "streaming," but when we compared notes, we loved all the same shows.

"What podcasts do you like?" he asked.

"I barely listen to any regularly," I replied, deciding this was the dealbreaker. I wasn't into many podcasts. "I like *The Daily* and this totally pointless inside-Hollywood thing with Jason Bateman, Sean Hayes and Will Arnett that's pretty funny."

"I love *SmartLess*. That's one of the few podcasts I never miss," he said as he reached for my hand and started caressing it. I quickly took a sip of wine and freed my hand from his.

He was interesting as well as interested in me. He's traveled the world to more than 30 countries and considers exploring other cultures as a key to a fulfilled life. I've left North America only twice, yet he wasn't the slightest bit condescending and wanted to know all about the state of journalism, my writing and teaching. Mr. Wrong Number did nothing wrong.

If we got married, we'd have the best ever how-we-met story and end up in *The New York Times*' "Vows" column telling the tale of the wrong number. Hilburn could officiate our wedding. They'd make a Hallmark movie about us. But I just wasn't feeling it.

He went to Budapest for ten days, and I replied to his texts less and less until they stopped. He was smart enough to realize the kismet gods were sadly wrong. He may well have felt the same.

After that, I made a conscious effort to enjoy the lack of responsibilities being solo brought and not think about dating. A few months later, the ex-wife of that old college crush I went out with after I first got divorced suggested I meet her neighbor. (You gotta love North Carolina.)

We have a lot in common, though he's an introvert and I'm an extrovert. He says it doesn't matter. We're good company and have fun going out here and there. There's a spark. But I'm not wearing his class ring around my neck, and neither of us foresee that.

Like most games, the dating game has unexpected twists and turns. You just have to keep going around the board and passing Go. If only you really did collect $200 each time.

— 16 —

I Killed Elvis

*I*t all started with a rat.

He spent his days nestled behind the wall in our pantry. I could hear him scratching whenever I fetched the Cheerios or Cheez-Its for the kids. While we slept, he emerged at night and ate holes in bags of rice and sugar. I'd awaken to find the grains and crystals that spilled on the floor along with some droppings the rat himself supplied for his late-night party.

Meanwhile, two houses away, my friend Caroline blamed her children first.

"Gross. Who ate half an avocado then smeared the other half all over the kitchen counter?" she yelled upstairs to Jack, Rose and Ellie when she saw the rat's crime scene one morning.

"I poured about 25 bottles of bleach on every inch of the counter, the floor, the furniture and the appliances," she told me after finding skinny-clawed rat footprints in the smeared green pool of evidence. "We will never eat guacamole again."

Our historic neighborhood with back alleys made of brick lined with giant trash dumpsters and picturesque citrus trees was besieged by rats who eagerly replied "yes" to the invite of the smell of rotting garbage and grapefruit. As soon as one was trapped, two more came to his funeral.

Jay, the Terminix technician, became such a regular at my house that our basset hound Delbert welcomed him with a wagging tail instead of the usual bellowing howl. I insisted that Jay hold Delbert in our Christmas card family photo that year.

Worse than finding the rats' half-eaten food and digestive remnants was finding a dead or half-dead rat in a sticky trap. Worse than that was finding a sticky trap with no rat but lots of rat hair next to the sofa.

"Look right here. See how the sofa is chewed up there?" Jay asked as he pointed to little holes and loose threads in the sofa skirt. "The rat must have dragged himself over here with one free leg, then pulled himself off the trap by biting on the sofa. He's hiding somewhere in the house. And I bet he's pretty freaked out."

So was I.

I immediately picked up my 3-year-old son Wade and stood up on the sofa. Then took a giant step over to the nearby table, which was higher. Jay searched every corner of the house with his flashlight but found nothing.

"Let's hope he managed to crawl back behind the wall or however else he's been coming and going," Jay said as he left.

That night after dinner the girls watched *Lizzie McGuire* and Wade played with blocks on the floor while I reported the day's events over the phone to my husband, who was out of town.

"Mommy. He got eyes," Wade called over to me. He was lying on his stomach staring under the armoire that held our TV.

"Who has eyes?"

"He do," Wade said, pointing to the darkness under the armoire.

I rushed over and looked down to see the beady eyes of a hideous rat who was possibly dead or half-dead. I swiped Wade up in my arms and screamed for Olivia and Charlotte to run upstairs, slammed the door to my bedroom and crammed at least nine towels in the half-inch space between the door and the floor. We all slept in my room with the TV going all night long in the family room. Jay came early the next morning and removed the almost dead carcass.

Finally, I got the city's pest control department to hang a plastic box full of who-knows-what across our backyard fence. Jay was good enough to also dispose of dead bodies in the yard. Finally, the rats ceased. Then came the fleas. Coincidence? I think not.

It was Hitchcockian. Over the years, when we'd find one or two fleas on Delbert's belly, I'd give him a NexGard chewable pill and the fleas were gone in a day.

This time they were everywhere. All over him. All over us. All over the furniture and the rugs.

"Mrs. Smith, I think we just need to bomb this place," Jay advised.

"Bring it on, Jay," I replied.

I had to get the children, Delbert and Elvis, the class guinea pig we were hosting for the summer, out of the house for eight hours. We spent a wonderful day at a friend's house out at the beach. Delbert slept on their cold tile floor keeping watch over Elvis in his cage while the humans frolicked in the hot tub that is the Gulf of Mexico in August.

At 4:30 p.m., I loaded up the children and livestock and headed back to our house 25 minutes away. Traffic was bad, so it took longer than expected and we went straight to Wade's swim class at a friend's pool. Alice's husband was out of town too, so we ordered pizza and had dinner over there after the class. That night I was reading a bedtime book to Wade when I remembered Elvis.

I'd taken Delbert inside Alice's yard during swimming and pizza, but totally forgot the guinea pig. Then I drove all of us home for baths and bedtime without the little guy crossing my mind.

"Elllllvissssss," I screamed, making Marlon Brando's "Stella" sound like a sweet whisper.

I raced down the stairs, rushed to the Honda Odyssey and flung open the back.

Elvis didn't move. I nudged his cage. Nothing.

Elvis was dead.

I killed Elvis.

Olivia, Charlotte and Wade were rushing across the yard. I met them a few feet before they reached the car and held them in my arms sobbing: "I'm so sorry. I'm so sorry. I am sooo, soo sorry."

We all cried our way inside and called Adam. He consoled us and calmed us down, telling the children Elvis was really old and about to die anyway. He told me it wasn't my fault. These things just happen. Then he asked me what I'd done with the body.

"It's still in the car in the cage," I said. "I just can't deal with that now. We can have a little funeral in the backyard when you get home."

"Well the car is going to start smelling pretty bad. I'm not going to be back for three more days. I know it's brutal, but you're going to have to get it out of there," he said.

"I'll call Kristin," I said. "She'll know what to do."

Kristin was our neighbor and good friend. She was part Harvey Keitel's The Wolf from *Pulp Fiction* and part Mary Poppins. She helped take care of things on our block of 18th Avenue NE where, at one point, our stretch of 10 houses between Locust and Poplar Streets was home to 21 children under 12.

Kristin cut the toddler boys' hair outside on the sidewalk then pointed our attention to the birds flying off with little tresses in their mouths to build nests. She could put a batch of strawberry scones in the oven then tear apart your resume and reconstruct it just as the oven timer rang. Kristin's job as a public relations consultant honed her crisis-control tactics. Her giving and upbeat nature made the crisis seem more like a little bump in the road.

Kristin was available to meet you on the sidewalk for a hug or strategy session as early as 5 a.m. and as late as midnight. (She was usually just coming in from or heading out on a run.)

I left Charlotte, Olivia and Wade in front of *Lizzie Mc-Guire* and called Kristin from another room to tell her what had happened.

"Okay. First of all, Katherine. This was not your fault. You keep so many plates in the air, some are going to fall sometime," she said. "Your children are safe. Delbert is safe. Class pets die all the time. Nobody else offered to take

Elvis. You did your part. He's in a better place."

She reminded me we'd already taken Elvis to the small animal vet twice that summer because he wasn't eating and had some strange lumps.

"Who knows? He might have had cancer, and this saved him from prolonged months of pain," she added.

And that's why Kristin is a public relations marvel.

"Alright. Now. Do you want to keep Elvis in your house or mine until Adam gets home?"

"This is a lot to ask, but can he stay at yours, please? I'd hate for the children to find him."

"Of course he can. I offered, didn't I?" Mary Poppins said with a reassuring laugh.

Within an hour she knocked on the door with a plate of hot sugar cookies and a sympathy card her two girls made for my children.

"Everything is taken care of and ready for the funeral Saturday," The Wolf whispered in my ear as she gave me a hug.

Elvis was buried in a shoebox covered in purple felt with his name written in gold sequins on the top. Along with making the casket, Kristin also cleaned out his cage and donated it to the local animal shelter in the name of my children's school.

By the time their school was back in session, my kids had accepted his death and went with Kristin's PR spin at school. Elvis died this summer from an illness that was exacerbated by the heat. None of the teachers complained about having one less animal cage to clean.

I think the experience still haunts me twenty years later because it's just one of many times I tried so hard to get everything right and it all went wrong. I suppose that's a lament of many parents, especially mothers. Even Kristin.

I have an oddly detailed memory for so many moments in my life. It enables me to write descriptively, even if I am unable to find my car in most parking lots these days. But I think all of us tend to remember the times we messed up more than when it all went as planned.

Another parenting debacle haunts me.

Charlotte, my middle child, took longer than expected to enunciate her words as a child. She was in speech therapy as a toddler and attended a preschool in the public school system that was taught by an actual speech therapist. There were only 10 kids in her class, and the fabulous instructor also had two wonderful teacher's aides. Furthermore, a big yellow school bus provided transportation to and from the half-day program.

A friend of a friend enrolled her son in the same program.

Jen was an ob-gyn with a new baby, and I was working part-time from home with a new baby. We also had our toddlers in the neighborhood church's preschool program in the mornings, so getting them to and from the preschool and the speech program in the afternoon was hard. With no family in town to help drive, it made total sense for our little kids to ride the bus.

Our decisions to stick Charlotte and her son Braden on a school bus raised some eyebrows in the era that was breeding the first generation of helicopter moms.

Jen and I still laugh whenever we run into each other at the grocery store or a party.

"You know all the other mothers thought we were the worst?" she says, leaning into a chuckle.

"Oh I know. Totally. Our kids were so little that the

stairs to get on the bus were half as tall as they were," I say with my voice cracking in laughter. "They could hardly climb up."

"All the other moms who were picking up their children from the morning preschool had a little snack and sippy cup waiting in the car. Then there's the grinding of the gears for the big yellow bus to pick up Charlotte and Braden," Jen recounts as we both double over.

The transportation arrangement, however, gave me one of my favorite stories about my daughter. A little boy in the neighborhood told Charlotte that he was in charge when they played on his swing set because he was three months older.

"Well, do you ride da school bus to school?" Charlotte asked defiantly. She knew she was one up on him with experience in the real world.

Her dual preschool program also led to that regrettable parent debacle. On the day of her Christmas show at the afternoon speech class, instead of having her take the bus, I picked her up from her morning preschool. I brought her freshly ironed red velvet jumper to change into for the afternoon show. Charlotte climbed in the minivan, squeezed her baby brother's hand, then settled into her own car seat.

"When we get to your other school you can change into your fancy dress for the Christmas show," I said as I buckled her in.

"I already had my show," Charlotte said. "Did you see it?"

"No, sweetie. Your show is this afternoon. We're going there now and Daddy is coming too." She may have said something after that, but I was racing to get to the next school on time and didn't listen.

I screeched into the afternoon school's parking lot and helped Charlotte change from the hot-pink Little Mermaid outfit into the velvet frock. Adam got there just in time for her group's song. Charlotte beamed when we cheered from the audience.

That night my friend Hope, whose son went to the morning school, called me.

"Katherine, you didn't know they had their Christmas concert this morning, did you?" she asked.

"Whaaaatttt?"

"Listen, I didn't want to tell you, but they're handing out a group photo tomorrow, so I knew you were going find out," Hope said. "It's okay. It happens to all of us."

"Oh my gosh. I went to all this effort to get her dressed up and be at the afternoon school's show, and then I totally missed the morning show. Poor Charlotte."

"Katherine, Charlotte was fine. I gave her a big hug after, and the kids weren't paying any attention to the parents. They had cookies. That's all they cared about."

"She was wearing a Little Mermaid swimsuit coverup to the Christmas show surrounded by girls in red velvet," I bemoaned.

"That's when I knew you'd forgotten," Hope said, with a little laugh. And I laughed.

"Look, I totally missed my son's teacher conference," she continued. "That's much worse. The teacher was waiting on me."

"Well at least you don't have to have a 5-by-7 photo of it," I said.

Eighteen years later, I was on deck for the very last school event for my three children. Wade was graduating from high school. I was far from grateful for a reprieve and wished we could rewind everybody to ten years earlier. My very last child was done with school and moving out in three months. I had plenty else to keep busy, including a j-o-b and aging parents. But seeing Wade graduate and leave was like closing the door on the childhood of all three of my children. That era of my life was over.

Graduations for St. Petersburg High School, as well as the 16 other public high schools in Pinellas County, take place at Tropicana Field, the indoor stadium where the Tampa Bay Rays play. The two-hour ceremonies are crammed up against each other over the course of two or three days between baseball games.

We were lucky that when Olivia and Charlotte graduated, their ceremonies were in the afternoon or early evening. But when Wade's turn rolled around, St. Pete High drew the short straw and got the first slot of the day: 7:30 a.m. That meant Wade had to leave home at 6 and be in place by 6:30 a.m.

It's a painful wake-up time for any class of high school seniors, but this was the class of 2021. These COVID kids had been dozing through online classes and making their own hours for half of their high school careers.

Wade was up for the challenge. There was some talk of his friends just staying up all night, but we parents somehow convinced them it would be better to try that the night after they graduate, not the night before.

Still, at the last minute, he decided to spend the night at his dad's condo downtown instead of my house because it was walking distance to the beach at the bay where his friends gathered the night before.

Fine by me. His green graduation gown hung in his room at my bungalow four miles away, and I promised to bring it to him by 5:45 the next morning.

My phone rang at 5:50 a.m.

"Mom! Where are you?" Wade asked in a panicked voice.

"I'm so sorry. I'm on my way," I said from my bed with my eyes barely open.

Whhaaatttt???? How did I mess up my alarm? This day, of all days????

I brushed my teeth. Threw on my dress. Stuffed a hairbrush and makeup in a bag. Grabbed the graduation gown and was out the door in under five minutes. It took another eight minutes to get to Adam's where he and Wade were waiting by the car at 6:10 a.m.

"Wade, I'm so sorry. I hate myself for messing up my alarm," I said. "But you've got plenty of time. It's going to be okay."

"Well, all my friends are already there so I won't be able to line up with them," Wade said. "But whatever. You had just one thing to do, Mom."

He drove his own car so he could leave with friends after the ceremony, and I rode in Adam's.

I understood Wade's frustration.

I do have a history of being five or ten minutes late. But never for important things like this. We've never missed a flight or even come close. And every child was there for the start of every soccer game, baseball game, lacrosse game, poetry slam, school play, debate team competition and Christmas pageant.

The traffic to Tropicana Field was bumper to bumper, which was good and bad. It meant Wade was going to be even later, but also that a lot of other students would be late too.

I called Wade.

"Why don't I jump in your car and wait in line to park, and you go on in?" I suggested.

"Mom. No. What if I can't find you later and I don't have my keys," he said. "I'll figure it out. I love you. It's okay," he said in a calmer tone.

As Adam and I walked into Tropicana Field around 7 a.m., students in green gowns were still racing past us. The Rays' home turf was barely half full when we found our seats around 7:15.

I caught my breath and ate the apple I'd thrown in my pocketbook as I ran out of the house. Then I looked down at my yellow dress and saw the seams and lining showing.

"I'm wearing my dress inside out," I said flatly to Adam.

"That's how you roll," he said with a smile.

Yes it is. It's how a lot of mothers roll. And we never have "just one thing to do," as Wade said. We're trying to kill the rats that brought the fleas that killed the guinea pig and iron red velvet dresses and sign the permission slips and attend the teacher conferences and get the wisdom teeth out and buy the flashcards for studying state capitals and make the birthday cake shaped like an alligator and race back to the craft store across town before it closes at 9 p.m. for more popsicle sticks for the model of the Japanese internment camps and pick up the Albuterol for the inhaler and find the signed blue cards for the next scouting rank and teach a badge in communications and sew a Caliban costume for *The Tempest* and fill the bathroom with steam at 3:30 a.m. when the barking cough won't stop and order the old tweed jacket off of Etsy for the Dr. Who Halloween costume and hound them for that last college essay.

We're the old ladies who swallow the spider to catch the fly, then go full throttle and choke down the bird, the cat, the dog, the goat and the horse. I don't know why we swallowed the fly. Maybe it came in on the rat.

And that's the wild ride we don't expect to board when that little baby is born, but we realize how incredibly lucky we are to have been on the always changing journey when the 18-year-old reaches for that diploma.

I'm at peace with my final score:

Guinea pigs: -1

Good human beings: 3

— 17 —

The Language of Family

I f I left the house as a teenager in just a cotton sweater on a 38-degree night, my mother always urged me to put on a coat.

Then my father countered with his usual catch phrase for nights when I didn't want to cover up the outfit I'd been perfecting for more than an hour.

"Her vanity will keep her warm," he said with a teasing glint in his deep-set eyes that were identical to mine.

This was one of many phrases in our family's shorthand. Our inside jokes.

If there was a lull in a conversation, Daddy would offer up an exuberant: "Well I fry mine in lard."

This phrase, which had no purpose except to fill a vacancy in dialog and bring a smile to those of us in the know, was born out of a church service in his childhood.

"The choir was singing away," he recounted as he explained his idiom's origin. "Two ladies on the front pew had been chatting during the entire hymn and didn't realize the singing had stopped. They must have been talking about chicken because the whole congregation heard one of the ladies loudly saying: 'Well I fry mine in lard.' "

I know my family isn't the only one with signature catch phrases that become a familiar and comforting part of an exclusive vocabulary.

Not long ago I was at the beach with my friend Hale and her husband, Michael. She and I sat on their deck overlooking Bogue Sound while he went inside to fetch us a glass of wine. It took him more than five minutes to return so I teased him.

"It took you long enough. I was about to leave my perch and get it myself."

"Just shaking the bush, boss," Michael said.

Hale laughed, but I had to ask for translation.

"It's from *Cool Hand Luke*," Michael explained. "That's what Paul Newman said when he took a bathroom break from the prison work crew. The guards would make them shake a bush the whole time so they knew they weren't trying to run away."

I learned about another family's secret code when I visited my friends Laura and Joe in Washington, DC, last year. Around 7 p.m., Laura and I took their black-lab-pit-bull mix named Daisy for a quick walk before we met Joe for dinner. As we left their patio on the way to walk her a couple quick blocks, Daisy looked longingly at the tennis ball with a crust of drool that sat on the round wrought-iron table.

"You don't always get a ball," Laura said to the dog.

"What's that all about?" I asked.

"We try to walk her three times a day. In the morning and after dinner, we take the ball and throw it for 10 minutes or so. In the middle of the day, it's quick, just a walk," Laura explained. "So Daisy knows the deal. She doesn't even think about the ball in the middle of the day. But if we don't take it in the morning or night, if there's not enough time, she stops at the table, hoping."

"Awww. I feel bad. I don't want our dinner to be the reason she doesn't get the ball tonight," I said.

"Oh, don't worry. She'll be okay," Laura assured me. "The funny thing is, the phrase has become a family joke when something doesn't work out like we hoped. The kids say, 'Sorry. You don't always get a ball.' I think it's partially a nod to Daisy and partially making fun of how matter-of-fact I can be."

My ex-husband and I still use a phrase I picked up when we were newly married. I shared it with him after overhearing two women in line for the bathroom of The Cactus Club in Tampa. One woman gripped her stomach and bemoaned, "I feel gross. I can't believe I ate three chicken enchiladas and all those chips."

Her friend countered chirpily, "Really? I just had a salad."

When our family eats together and Adam or I comment on the delicious dessert or rich pasta, the other usually quips, "I wouldn't know. I just had a salad."

Another exchange in our marriage resulted in a favorite abuse of language in my parents' home.

One Saturday, Adam bought a few hibiscus bushes and asked me to call our friend and neighbor Gretchen to come over and help decide where he should plant them.

"I want to ask for Gretchen's opinion before I do anything," he said. Gretchen is a lawyer, not a horticulturist, but has great taste.

"Can you walk over sometime today to give us your good opinion on where to plant some hibiscus bushes?" I asked her on the phone. She promised to stop by within a couple hours.

Wade, who was about 4 or 5 at the time, was listening intently to all this hibiscus talk.

"Is Gretchen the same as Mrs. Walsh?" he asked.

"That's right. Henry's and Duncan's mother."

"When is she coming over?"

"In an hour or two. But she's not bringing the boys. We just need to get her opinion."

Within 20 minutes Wade was looking out the window for our friend. He asked me to call Gretchen again. His eagerness was a little confusing, but also sweet. I didn't realize she was one of his favorite neighborhood moms.

Finally, Gretchen knocked on the door, having already surveyed our yard and come up with two options. Wade rushed ahead of Adam and me as we walked outside.

Gretchen presented her opinion in a logical, analytical way, stating the pros and cons in regard to sunlight, groundcover, curbside appeal and ease of watering.

I gave her a Diet Coke and a hug. She made no mention of billable hours and headed for the sidewalk to leave.

Wade, who had been patiently digging in the dirt with a stick, looked up with panic on his little face.

"Wait, Mrs. Walsh. Where's your opinion?" he called after her.

She offered a confused smile, and I asked him what he meant.

"You said you were going to get her opinion," he explained. "You know, with all the candy inside. Like at a birthday party."

And that's when my parents began saying, "I need to get your piñata on something."

Many signature sayings spring from experiences that are distinct to a family, a couple or friends. But some of my personal favorites in my childhood to adulthood are colloquial phrases from my parents' upbringing.

My mother says, "Lord willin' and if the creek don't rise," when she promises to do something or see us soon.

Daddy's highest compliment was: "It's better than snuff."

He wasn't sure from where it derived. Likely, older ladies who dabbled in the sweet-smelling ground tobacco used it as the highest benchmark.

When you were getting close to finishing a project, a long drive or any task, both my parents said, "We're getting to the short rows." This comes from working on a farm where the rows were more uneven and shorter at the end of the field.

Daddy also adopted his aunts' and uncles' trademark reply when someone asked, "How are you today?"

"Tolerable," they'd say. "Tolerable."

I heard Daddy and my Aunt Ann share this exchange my whole life. They got a chuckle out of how their elders in the old days didn't want to let on when things were going fine, or perhaps when they weren't. "Tolerable" was a general enough statement.

In the final months of my father's life, he and Aunt Ann would sit hearing-aid-to-hearing-aid on her yellow-flowered living room sofa. They were both in their mid- to late-90s, and they could barely hear each other. She was in almost constant pain and slept a lot. Still, he always asked how she was feeling.

"Tolerable," Aunt Ann would answer with a sly smile. "And how are you, A.C.?"

"Tolerable. I suppose I'm tolerable," he'd say and pat her leg.

Even when you can barely hear the language of your family, you still know what it means.

Love.

— 18 —

Brutal War, Beautiful Words

Two weeks after my father died at the age of 97, I met him again as the 19-year-old soldier he'd been in World War II. Under a file of important letters and a few issues of *Sports Illustrated* with the Tar Heels on the cover, I found the journal he kept from his time in the war.

I grew up knowing him as a very supportive and loving father, then later understood more of his role as the editor of *The Raleigh Times* and longtime columnist for that paper as well as *The News & Observer*. Reading his journal, I glimpsed his young mind and got a firsthand look at the lives of so many of that Greatest Generation.

My father was drafted about a year after graduating from Dobson High School in Surry County. He served in the US Army Air Corps, which was the aerial warfare component of the army and later became the US Air Force. He was stationed at Seymour Johnson Air Force Base in North Carolina when he learned on December 31, 1943, that he was heading overseas. He left a week later by train for California.

His journal begins on January 1, 1944: "I never thought I'd really go." The final page from November 17, 1945, reads: "I Am A Civilian!"

Along with the handwriting I recognize so well, the journal is filled with his eloquent way of describing scenes of life that many people, certainly most 19-year-old boys, overlook.

On January 14, 1944, ironically the same day and month that decades later my sister was born and that decades after that Daddy would die, he wrote of leaving the United States as he boarded a barge in Pittsburg, California, for the USS *Monticello*, the troop carrier that would transport him across the Pacific.

"Civilians waved goodbye. I was impressed by an old man and gray-haired woman standing together waving frantically. The fellows around me laughed. But I knew that these two old people were sincere in their emotions."

My Aunt Ima, one of my father's 16 siblings, is identified on the first page as the one who gave him the journal.

The book's pages came with prompts like "My Buddies in the Service," "Officers I Have Met," "Gifts I Have Received" and "Autographs" to help kick-start uncertain writers. It stopped short of saying "War Can Be Fun."

There are postage-stamp-sized sketches of jolly servicemen playing the harmonica, waving to pals or shaking hands with a lovely woman. The bottom of each page has an inspiring, often pro-war quote from Shakespeare, Theodore Roosevelt and the Bible.

The page eliciting "Places I Have Been" has a sketch of a serviceman on a city street. My father added the word "Stationed" after "Been." He lists nine islands in the South Pacific with short descriptions such as "terrible," "still worse" and "muddy." He calls Okinawa "hell." The island of Pugo receives the only high marks: "paradise."

He was never in direct combat but "guns roared" all around as Japan tried to take over the islands the Allies occupied. Ultimately my father was assigned to Communications, which included working with secret codes, manning the switchboard and flying with pilots to other islands to retrieve soldiers or take supplies.

One of the earliest entries, while he was still stateside, is from January 6, 1944: "The morning of Jan. 6 about 400 soldiers were gathered at the Parade Ground with packs and gas masks. We shivered in the early morning dampness until at 10 o' clock, when we began to march to the railroad accompanied by a big band."

After a week on the train, he boarded the *Monticello* troop carrier for the 18-day trip across the ocean.

January 17, 1944: "From 10:30 a.m. to 12:30 p.m. we are allowed on deck. The hours we look forward to each day. Usually Charlie, Don and I just stare at the endless ocean and discuss anything and everything. These are the shortest hours of the day. The heat is blistering, but at least we get some fresh air. Twice today we spotted ships, and the alarm was given, but I was relieved to find they were Allies."

A few weeks later: "On the early morning of Feb. 3, we saw land. We were all elated and thronged to the deck. We were told this was New Guinea. It looked very green and jungle-like. We had thought all along we were going to Australia. Not one of us had ever even heard of this place, and not one had any desire to get off here. ... We reached the shore. Two abreast we started marching, expecting to be massacred by the Japanese at any moment. After walking an hour, a truck came along and picked us up. We jostled along for 15 miles and finally stopped. We piled off and were led down to a row of tents. Some fellow asked me where I was from and I was so tired and discouraged I announced: 'America,' at which he mumbled 'smart guy.' ... No one had told us a thing and we knew not what to expect."

After reaching the island of New Guinea in the South Pacific, he was attacked by ants in his cot, which sat in waist-high grass. But the next morning he described the sunrise.

February 4, 1944: "The sun arose from behind a nearby mountain. It was a crimson ball of fire, which turned the cloudless sky into a spectrum of colors. The tall leaves of the coconut palms seemed to be waxed, and the water in the bay shimmered in the early dawn while the jungle birds awakened and began screaming and flying about."

On New Guinea his squadron built much of the Milne Bay base as the Allies occupied the large island and fought against the Japanese to maintain control.

March 12, 1945: "Some days we work 4 p.m. to midnight. Others from 11 p.m. to 8 a.m. We work every day, Sundays and all. We unload ships, work with cranes, clear the jungle, build latrines and everything else imaginable."

As I read these words, my heart ached for my father and all the men and women from all the wars who ended up in faraway lands where they had no idea what lay ahead. I thought about how much times have changed. One of the days I spent digesting his journal through tears and smiles,

I received an email from my son's university. Wade, also age 19, was about to complete his first year of college and sign up for sophomore housing.

"Understand that this is often a stressful process for students. Though the process is simple, the social-emotional stress of choosing roommates and making decisions about the future can make a simple process feel fraught," the director of housing wrote.

I truly appreciate a school that cares about its students, but this attitude is light years from what young people faced going off to war. In the 14 days it took for my father and his fellow soldiers to cross the Pacific Ocean, nobody even informed them where they were going to end up. And this, of course, is why the 16 million men—and 350,000 women—who fought in World War II are considered the Greatest Generation. They did what they were called to do with no questions asked. They fought and worked in extreme heat and cold, survived on mediocre food and found solace in their friendships and the occasional simple pleasures. Going to a church service was a treat, as was a Betty Grable movie, or the chance to wash their clothes in a creek on the first afternoon off in three weeks. Letters from relatives, friends and even teachers were recorded regularly in my father's journal. He read them "over and over again."

He writes of a few other lighter moments.

March 12, 1945: "One time Don, Charlie and I worked in a warehouse and did nothing but race up and down on loading machines. ... We had movies three nights a week. The theater was only logs lined up on a hill surrounded by the jungle with the screen up front. Natives climbed the trees at the edge of the jungle and watched the miracles of movies. The Red Cross did a swell job. They furnished us with lemonade."

My father wasn't in direct combat, so clearly he had it easier than many. But he was still exposed to death, or the near death of others, regularly.

May 16, 1944: "I watched the crew of a B-24 jump out of their plane. Heard the pilot over the radio receiver. He put the automatic pilot on. It flew into the clouds to be later shot down."

September 6, 1944: "My good friend and fellow student Logan has been killed. He's the first of our [high school] class to die and the last, I hope."

September 27, 1944: "A 171 fighter squadron plane crashed. 9 people killed. Lt. Jameson, Nash Fredericks and Dale Garrett were killed. The whole tent went to the funeral."

November 17, 1945, Fort Bragg: "At 10:17 tonight I received the papers that set me free. ... It seems so long ago that I came in. Parts of this life were really ok. Other parts weren't. I've met the finest type of Americans. I've tried to remember the good and forget the bad. Well, I'll close this now, hoping that civilian life will not be too harsh on me."

His family was fortunate. Three of his brothers and four of his nephews served in World War II. They all came back alive.

I wonder if Charlie and Don made it, and if they did, I wonder where their civilian lives took them. I know Lt. Jameson, Nash Fredericks and Dale Garrett perished. I'd like to try to find descendants of all of them and tell them their father or uncle meant something to my young father at a time when he was lonely and scared.

— 19 —

Every, Every Minute

The social worker from Transitions, Raleigh's hospice program, admired the magenta crepe myrtle in my parents' backyard.

"I think it's more brilliant this year than ever before," my 96-year-old father said.

Though he was far from needing hospice, somebody had told me to establish a relationship with Transitions so when the time did come, we'd already have the paperwork done and be in the system.

For decades, my parents had had living wills that dictated they didn't want extreme measures taken to keep them alive if death loomed. Ironically the appointment I booked a month earlier for my dad came up on the calendar when my mother, who was seven years younger, was unexpectedly in the hospital recovering nicely from a broken hip.

So it was just me on the porch with my father when the Transitions counselor was seeking more specifics on end-of-life decisions.

"Would you want a feeding tube to keep you alive if you are near the end of life?" she asked.

"I'm sorry. I've still got my marbles, but my hearing has all but deserted me," Daddy replied. "Can you please speak a little louder?"

When he heard the question, he looked at me to get my thoughts.

"A feeding tube sounds like extreme measures, Daddy. But it's up to you."

"That's right. I wouldn't want a feeding tube," he declared.

"Next question. Would you want to be given antibiotics if an infection would end your life without them?" she asked.

"Yes," he said without hesitation.

"Would you want to be resuscitated by a device that delivers an electric shock to stimulate the heart?" she continued.

"Hmmmm," Daddy mused this one and looked at me again. I shrugged. It was his decision. "Yes. I think so," he said.

I loved him so completely at this moment. For at least ten years, he'd been saying he was too old to buy green bananas because he might not last until they ripen. But here at 96 and with bad hearing, he valued every day, every human interaction, the song from every wood thrush, the cool taste of every Klondike bar and thought the crepe myrtle was the best it had ever been.

Of course, I loved him at every moment. He'd been a constant, wonderful force in my life since I was a little girl, and I only appreciated him more each year.

Along with giving me a heart that perhaps is too sensitive, he showed me how humor heightens the joy, helps with the pain and makes the in-between better.

"He checked yes to almost everything except being cryogenically frozen," I said to my cousin, Lynn, when she visited with Daddy and me on the porch later that day.

"Lynn, I should have you in charge of all this. I can't trust Katherine because she might just want to run off with all my riches," he teased me back.

"Well, Uncle A.C., the Snows do not go gentle into that good night, do they?" asked Lynn.

"No we don't. 'Rage, rage against the dying of the light,'" Daddy said, reciting another line from Dylan Thomas.

He recalled how his brother Roosevelt, who was Lynn's grandfather, always said the family came from "good stock." Of 16 children born to Ida Victoria and Bird Winfield Snow, one died of leukemia in her 30s and another from a heart attack in his 40s. The rest lived into their 90s. One of Daddy's brothers painted the exterior of his house a few days before he died. It drove my father crazy when his oldest nephew, my first cousin, bragged at the annual Snow reunion that he was still mowing his own yard and taking no medication except a daily aspirin at age 94.

My father, who was the youngest of the family, said he made it to "the final four" when only he, his sister Zetta and brothers Warren and Arvel remained. By the time we sat on the porch that day, only he was left. At the last Snow reunion in Yadkinville there was literally a line of relatives waiting to take a picture with the family patriarch.

"I hate to tell you, but these photos aren't going to be worth anything on eBay when I die," Daddy joked.

His "good stock" as well as connection with loyal readers enabled him to write his human-interest column until the age of 95.

Though Daddy joked about his age, he never really considered himself old. When the good people of Edenton Street United Methodist Church delivered meals three days a week to older members during COVID, Daddy, at age 95, worried they should be concentrating their efforts on "the old folks who really need help."

There was a time much earlier when I worried he and my mother would actually give up on life. They were devastated when my older sister and their beloved first born, Melinda, died in a car accident at age 31 on Father's Day. My parents' friends, faith and love for each other brought them through the haze and horror in the months that followed her death, though nothing would ever fill the gaping hole.

A good friend of mine got married in Raleigh on the one-year anniversary of Melinda's death. We were invited to a brunch the morning of her wedding day at the same venue where my parents hosted my wedding reception four years earlier. It was going to be hard for us to be back at this place that was filled with good memories of Melinda alive, dancing with my dad and giving a beautiful, witty toast. My mother stayed home with Olivia, my 6-month-old daughter, but my father insisted he felt up to going to the brunch with me. He hugged Ellen, the bride, and talked with her parents, but we didn't stay long.

We rode down in the elevator with Frank Daniels Jr., the publisher of the paper where Daddy worked. My dad's longtime boss and friend asked how I liked working for the *St. Petersburg Times*. I said it was great, and Daddy told him he loved reading the paper when he visited Florida but hated having to fly to get there.

"Even though I was in the air force in World War II and was a passenger in tiny prop planes all across the South

Pacific, I've come to fear flying," he admitted.

"What are you afraid of, A.C.?" Frank Jr. asked with his signature bluntness.

"The plane going down," Daddy replied loudly as though it was obvious.

"Well, A.C., how much longer do you think you've got anyway?" Frank Jr. countered.

"Apparently a lot longer than you think I'm entitled to," my father huffed. He was 72 at the time and only eight years older than his boss but perhaps looked more senior with his salt-and-pepper hair that was more salt than pepper.

Twenty minutes later Daddy and I were in the car, almost home, and he fumed: "Who the hell does Frank Jr. think he is? I may just outlive him."

I knew at that moment he and my mom were going to be okay. Their lives had been gutted with Melinda's death, but they knew they still had much to live for.

Ten years later I was sitting alone on their porch on the night of Father's Day. I had dropped both of my daughters at Camp Seafarer on the North Carolina coast that morning. My youngest, Wade, who wasn't old enough for camp, was inside mesmerized by his Mimi reading Dr. Seuss's *Gertrude McFuzz* to him.

I watched the lightning bugs flicker across our backyard, thinking of June nights that smelled just like that one when Melinda and I caught the glowing insects and imprisoned them in an empty jelly jar with holes punched in the lid. A summer rain started pounding, and I hoped the noise would camouflage my crying as I let loose.

I guess it didn't. Daddy came out to the porch and hugged me as I sobbed harder.

"How are you not so sad?" I asked him.

"Of course I get sad. Some days, for no apparent reason, are much harder than Father's Day," he said. He went on to say his own version of a cup half full instead of half empty. It wasn't rocket science, but it has stuck with me.

"Losing Melinda was and is horrible. I miss her desperately every day. But I've also had a lot of good in my life. Having Melinda was a gift. Having you and your children is a gift. I still have a good life."

He did have a good life. But he also had a good way of looking at life.

Like many men and women of the Greatest Generation born between 1920 and 1925 who grew up during the Great Depression, Daddy knew what it was like to be extremely poor as a child and then feel like his life could easily end as a teenager in a war. He gained an early respect for life's gifts, big and small.

His siblings, many of whom had children of their own by the time my father was born, would tell Melinda and me when we were kids that our father was spoiled because he was the baby of the family. The evidence: he got jelly on his biscuit.

After he graduated as salutatorian of his class at Dobson High School in 1942, Daddy worked 11 different odd jobs for a few months from soda jerk to the commissary manager at a textile mill until he was drafted into the US Army Air Corps. The Pacific was the first ocean he ever saw as he crossed it in a troop carrier headed for World War II. He soon joined other teenagers and young men who shared tents with snakes and mosquitoes as they island-hopped from New Guinea throughout the South Pacific. They buried friends who died on the islands, as well as enemies who washed up on shore, in sandy graves marked with crosses made of palm fronds.

Like many of his generation, he rarely mentioned the war to his children and grandchildren. When he did, he shared the rare good times. One Christmas his mother sent him a pair of shoes because basic supplies were allowed to pass through the overseas mail service more quickly than cookies or candy. When Daddy opened the box on Christmas Eve, he found a bottle of Coca-Cola wrapped in newspaper within each shoe. He passed the bottles around his tent, and his buddies took long swigs with eyes closed.

"It tasted like home," he told us.

Daddy was in Tokyo a few days after the war ended, celebrating with elated friends. Each held up a pack of cigarettes, which had been unavailable in Japan for several years, and sold them for enough money to finance a six-course meal at Frank Lloyd Wright's Imperial Hotel. The GI Bill paid for college.

He started at Mars Hill College near Black Mountain, North Carolina, and corresponded for years after he left with excellent teachers, including one who taught him all about classical music. Daddy told us funny stories of the school's strict rules. Housemothers patrolled the parlors in the girls' dorms with a ruler, making sure the males—who had been all over the world living on their own during a war with few rules—were always sitting 6 inches apart from the females.

His sophomore year, word spread across campus that some girls were sunbathing topless up in the cemetery. The male students didn't dare go up there, though they were tempted. But the male dean of students rushed to disperse the scandalous behavior.

"He was so determined not to see the topless girls, he backed his car up the hill and got out with his hand over his eyes to admonish them," Daddy said, laughing, decades later.

After two years at Mars Hill, he went on to UNC and graduated in 1950 as a member of Phi Beta Kappa. He described Carolina as "Camelot" in an essay published in a book that the university released with alumni memories on the school's 200th birthday.

With a journalism degree and the guidance of a favorite UNC professor, he got his first job at the *Burlington Times-News*.

"He's not much to look at, but he's a fine writer," Professor Stuart Sechriest told the paper's editor when he drove his star student over for an interview.

After a few years in Burlington, he got a job as a reporter at *The Raleigh Times* covering city hall, then went on to be a city editor, managing editor and editor-in-chief. All along the way my father wrote a human-interest column. His trademark style would later be described by *The News & Observer* reporter Josh Shaffer as "country wisdom wrapped in elegant prose."

One summer I interned in the dispatch office of *The News & Observer* and *The Raleigh Times*, driving proofs of ads around to advertisers to get their edits and final approval. I rode to the office each morning with my father, who arrived by 6 a.m. because the afternoon paper went to press midday. My job didn't start until 9 a.m., so we kept a blanket and pillow in Daddy's lower left desk drawer so I could snooze on a small club chair in the corner of his office before my day started. I remember as I write this that when I was in and out of slumber, Daddy came and went from his office amidst the stress of getting the paper out and tucked the blanket up around my shoulders if it slipped.

He went to lunch at Belk's cafeteria most days with "the boys," which is what he called his colleagues and good friends Mel, Dave and John.

On the walk to my first lunch with the group, Jim Martin, who was governor at the time, passed us and stopped Daddy to discuss an editorial he'd written. "The boys" exchanged pleasantries with the governor and walked ahead. Though I stayed back, my father didn't introduce me to the governor, and I was a little annoyed. But when we got to the cafeteria line, he proudly introduced me to each person serving the roast beef, fried okra, banana pudding and sweet tea. He knew them by name, where they were from and the other jobs they worked or the school they attended. He meant no offense to the governor when he didn't introduce us, but the people he counted as friends, not government officials, were the ones he wanted me to meet.

It's obvious I unabashedly adored my father. My biggest frustration with him would be that even though I visited Raleigh from Florida about once a month for the last decade of his life, whenever he saw me roll out my suitcase to depart he'd say, "Oh no. It's leaving time again. Katherine, it seems like you just got here." The last six months of his life, I was living in Chapel Hill and I saw him every other day. He'd still say the same thing when I hugged him goodbye.

But he wasn't perfect, of course. For all his love of life he had a curmudgeonly side. If Carolina fell more than 6 points behind in basketball, he'd have to turn down the volume. A 10-point deficit sent him out of the house to rake leaves or walk around the block. If it was nighttime, he'd retire to bed only to have my mother call him back out when the Heels had the lead.

He and "the boys" from the office rented a condo at the beach to watch the ACC tournament for many years. One year Daddy stomped to his room when Carolina fell behind in the championship game. The boys, led by the mischievous Dave, booed and hissed as they retired to their rooms, even though the Heels had won. They hid the newspaper the next day and told Daddy his team lost a 20-point lead in the last five minutes of the game. This was pre-Internet so my father had no idea. He could barely buoy himself to go out to lunch, where they ran into some happy Carolina fans and he realized his friends had been fooling him all day.

My father was 41 when Melinda was born and 44 when I arrived. He said he was glad to have girls because he was too old to toss a football with a son. He was 72 when his first grandchild, Olivia, came into our world. He worried again he was too old to be a good grandfather, but he was. Both my parents were very involved with her, with Charlotte who came two years later, and with Wade four years after that. They took them to the NC State Fair, drove them to pumpkin patches, came to St. Petersburg for school plays and baseball games. At age 75, Daddy even climbed into the overhead tunnels in a McDonald's to retrieve a shoe Olivia had lost up there.

"If I had known how filthy it was up there, I would have just let her turn into a pumpkin," he groused, with a wink at her and a nod to Cinderella's lost slipper.

We all went on a *Queen Mary II* cruise twice when my kids were in their teens and and took three Disney cruises when they were younger. After we left the last Disney cruise, we claimed our luggage in the hot warehouse in the cruise terminal and were eager to get in the car for the two-hour drive home. One problem: my husband Adam couldn't find the car keys.

"I swear I gave them to you," he said as we both dumped out our suitcases while my parents and children waited patiently. Eagle-eyed Olivia spotted Rondell Sheridan, who was the father on *That's So Raven* as well as a standup comedian on the cruise. She asked for his autograph, which he grudgingly gave. Finally, Adam found the car keys in the outside pocket of his suitcase.

On the drive home, my camp-counselor side emerged, along with my good-daughter side. I suggested we all go around and share our "most magical moment," an overused Disney phrase. Also, my parents had paid for the trip, so I wanted them to hear what it meant to everyone.

My children delivered fabulously with fun moments each shared with their grandparents. My father offered up no sentimental musings, saying, "The most magical moment for me was when Adam found his keys and we could go home."

The curmudgeon in him made my children laugh. The naturalist in him showed them how to sit as still as statues in our backyard as his beloved bluebirds ate live mealworms out of his flat palm raised toward the sky. As with his readers, he gave his friends and family doses of reality and humor, as well as a feeling that we are special and lucky to be alive.

The last time Daddy and I were together I flew into Raleigh after he was already asleep. He fell in the night and didn't have the strength to pull himself back up. A wonderful caregiver and I tried, but we couldn't help him either.

"We just need to call those nice firemen. They've been here once before to help," my mother said. The heroes arrived in the full truck and ladder and gingerly lifted Daddy into his bed as if he was a feather. He caught his breath and amidst all the chaos reached to squeeze my hand and gave me an official greeting: "Hey Katherine. How was your flight?"

The firemen heard crackling in his congested lungs and measured low oxygen saturation. They wanted to take him to the hospital for an IV and oxygen supply. My mother looked at me and shook her head sadly. We didn't want him to suffer the discomfort and upheaval of moving to a hospital. He had grown very weak in the past few days. We sensed the end was near.

I stood in my childhood bedroom where he read to me as a little girl, the room where he would see my 4-year-old emerging independence and defiance and turn on the overhead "big light," as I called it, so I could look at books after he'd already read me several and turned off the light. In that room, under the same big light, I told the firemen through tears that we didn't want any medical intervention. My mother had gone to the kitchen to get the yellow Do Not Resuscitate papers taped to the corner of the refrigerator.

Those nice firemen didn't try to persuade us but told me as his health-care power-of-attorney to fingerpaint my name across an electronic screen acknowledging that I refused transport to the hospital.

Six months had passed since Daddy sat on the porch with the Transitions counselor checking the boxes wanting intervention so he could live each new day. He'd grown weaker and more dependent on others, but thankfully, still had his "marbles."

The Transitions hospice team arrived the next day and set up a hospital bed in our family room. Daddy settled in, next to a bank of windows overlooking our big backyard, which had plagued him every fall for 60 years when falling oak leaves demanded endless raking. In spring, it delighted him with jonquils blooming on the edge of the woods and bluebirds building nests in the many houses he leased to them.

Daddy walked from the hospice bed to the dinner table that evening and said a prayer.

"Thank you God for each day you see fit to give us. Please be with Nancy, Katherine and the children, and all those who are suffering."

He declared his strawberry milkshake from Chick-fil-A one of the best he'd ever had.

My mother and I slept on sofas on either side of him. He moaned some in his sleep, so I started putting drops of morphine under his tongue every four hours as the hospice nurse had shown me. He didn't talk at all the next day but squeezed our hands as my mom and I held his. Hospice nurses and various friends advised us to assure him we'd be alright if he moved on. My mother and I shared several renditions of gratitude and love, but he lived through the night. The next day, he didn't talk or wake up and his breathing became more labored. We reassured him more. Then I talked to him for the first time about Olivia, Charlotte and Wade and shared how well they were doing in their various points of life.

He took his last breath twenty minutes later.

At his funeral, Charlotte read "Dust of Snow," his favorite Robert Frost poem.

For my part, I recounted taking my children to see a production of *Our Town* in St. Petersburg several years earlier. As we left the theater, I asked them if the final conversation between Emily and the stage manager reminded them of anyone.

"SnowDaddy," Olivia said, and Wade and Charlotte agreed they were thinking the same thing.

In the play's final scene, a twenty-something Emily has died but is allowed to come back and relive one day with her family in her beloved hometown of Grover's Corners. She picks her twelfth birthday but finds it too hard to watch and asks the stage manager, who seems to oversee such things, if they could leave the land of the living. Emily bids a final farewell to life in Grover's Corners along with the beautiful mundane occurrences like clocks ticking, sunflowers blooming, the smell of coffee and hot baths. She asks the stage manager if humans ever realize all life gives them "every, every minute" when they are alive.

The stage manager sadly says, no, except for maybe a few saints or poets.

Robert Frost knew a crow landing on a hemlock tree in a snowy wood triggering a dust of snow could change the mood of a whole day. He was one of those poets.

My father was far from a saint or a poet, but he did appreciate life. Just about every, every minute of it.

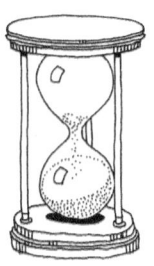

— 20 —

With My People

The day before my father's funeral, frost dusted the grass at the cemetery, but the January ground wasn't frozen. When I pushed the wire stem of the small blue plastic flag into the ground to mark his burial plot, it entered the earth easily. The cemetery manager explained to me that a family member is asked to mark it to safeguard against anyone being buried in the wrong place. He provided me with a map and contract showing the site my parents had bought decades earlier.

I knew without the paperwork that this was the spot because of the grave to the left.

The marker read "GLAD2BEME" in bronze letters beneath my sister's name: Melinda Jean Snow. The phrase had appeared on her personalized license plate. She died at age 31 in a car accident. Daddy died 25 years later of pneumonia on her birthday, January 14.

"So then your mother will go right there on the right of your father when her time comes," the manager said as he pointed to a plot on the right of where I planted my father's little plastic flag.

"This is a tough time to be thinking about this, but is there any room around here for me?" I asked, surveying the hilltop that seemed filled with tombstones and markers. "I got divorced a few years ago so I guess I no longer have a plan for where I'll end up."

"I doubt it, but let's go back to the office and check," he said. Shockingly, there was one space available next to my sister's and parents' plots. I plan to be cremated, but he said I could have a marker and my ashes there. I told him I'd decide after I got through my father's funeral.

Like my parents, I'm not one to frequent cemeteries. They placed flowers on Melinda's grave on every birthday but weren't regulars. A neighbor down the street drove past our house every afternoon on his way to his wife's grave.

"There goes Bob to visit Marion," Daddy would say. "Must be 5 o'clock."

We didn't talk much about death, but my father said from time to time he was fond of the phrase the Irish used when proposing marriage: "Will you be buried with my people?"

The storied family burial grounds aren't as common now as families disperse thousands of miles beyond their original village, town, state or country.

As a child I explored the headstones of members of my father's family at the cemetery at Snow Hill Baptist Church in Dobson, North Carolina. During summer visits to his Surry County birthplace, Daddy took Melinda and me to the graves of his parents and other relatives. He and I took my son, Wade, on the same sojourn decades later. It was more of a history lesson than a somber memorial.

Daddy wanted us to understand how unusual it was that my grandfather, Byrd Winfield Snow, was born in 1862 during the Civil War. My grandmother, Ida Victoria Snow, whose middle name is the same as mine, was born 20 years later. Together they raised 16 children, my father being the youngest. His father was 64 when my father was born, then he didn't become a father to Melinda until he was 41, and to me at 44. So that's how the math works for children born in the 1960s to have a grandfather born during the Civil War.

Wade and I took photos at the graves belonging to great, great uncles, Frost Snow and Ice Snow, who moved to Surry County from England in the early 1800s. Daddy was proud of the humor in the family tree.

Beyond names on headstones, people's many different preferences for how they will be laid to rest are interesting, and at times, even humorous.

A friend recounted the story of an eccentric man in his small town who asked to be placed face down in his casket so that when people paid their respects they could "kiss my ass goodbye."

My oldest daughter, Olivia, led me to the Westwood Village Memorial Park during a visit to Los Angeles. She had researched the celebrities buried there and knew some lore.

Marilyn Monroe's crypt is usually covered with kisses made by red lipstick from the lips of fans paying their respects. Hugh Heffner, founder of *Playboy* magazine, bought the crypt next to her so he would eventually be laid to rest beside the famous beauty who appeared on the cover of the first issue of his magazine.

Talk show host Merv Griffin is also buried at Westwood.

His gravestone reads, "I will NOT be back right after these messages."

Roosevelt, one of the oldest of my father's 15 siblings, had his gravestone erected several years before he died. It was one of the biggest markers in the small cemetery next to his church in Dobson. Roosevelt liked to drive by and admire it. He purposely picked a plot near the edge so it was visible from the road, and he joked his family members could just drive by and toss flowers right over the fence.

He and his wife, Eva, were married 73 years. When the two were in their 90s, my father asked his sister-in-law if she ever dated anyone else before she married Roosevelt.

"Yes, I did. Two different young men. They're both dead now," she said matter-of-factly. "I should have married one of them."

Though they bickered, they were devoted to each other. When Roosevelt died, Eva wanted a living room chair placed by the window facing the cemetery so she could look out toward him every day until she was buried next to him.

A few weeks after my father died, I went back to the Raleigh cemetery and bought the plot next to my parents and sister. I told the cemetery manager that I remembered the headline of a column my dad wrote decades ago when he and my mom first bought their plots that read: "It's Not Like Bringing a New Baby Home."

"He sure was right about that," I said.

"Everybody in this town loved your father," the manager said, "because no matter their politics, their profession or whatever, he said what people were thinking so much of the time."

He went on to tell me about how at least 15 years earlier, the former cemetery director was so proud of a fancy new sign with a digital screen that flashed the time and temperature.

"Well, your daddy called up here and said he thought it was in poor taste and that this was a place of peace and reflection not a bank, a sports arena or a Las Vegas hotel. Nobody wants the time and temperature flashing all night long," the manager said. "He was right. A lot of people were complaining to me about the clock, but your father was the only one calling the director. Finally, our boss came in one day and said, 'Mr. Snow has worn me down. If he puts this in his column the whole town's gonna be after me. I'm shutting down the clock.'"

This story was a gift as I wrote the check for my cemetery plot. I laughed and felt such a closeness to Daddy.

I don't know the right words to describe the pain my parents felt when they had to purchase a cemetery plot for Melinda long before her time. I will call them brave and strong for going on to live good, meaningful lives even as they missed her tremendously. They could be content knowing they raised Melinda and me to be "GLAD2BME." I hope I somehow manage the same for my children.

I take comfort knowing no matter where my uncertain life takes me, I'll be buried with my people. And no time or temperature will be flashing all night long.

— Afterword —

When I started this book in 2021, the word "untethered" rang frequently in my mind. My last child had just left for college, my work was remote, and I felt more out of place than I had predicted coming back to North Carolina. Six months later when my father died, that uneasy feeling of not knowing my real place or purpose transformed to an awful directionless emptiness. I kept seeing the helium balloons that my children were always given on grocery store trips go hurtling into the sky when they accidentally let go of the string in the parking lot. I felt so helpless when all we could do was just watch the speck of blue or green fly off with no direction or landing spot until it disappeared from sight. I was that balloon.

The constant in my life, the best person in my life, the person who loved me more than anyone else, was gone.

But a chance encounter four months later with someone I know because of my father led to a solid landing, and a new path and purpose. Now, as much as my father influenced my work in journalism, my mother is the inspiration I follow in my next career.

I'm teaching and I love it. I'm also going back to college at UNC-Chapel Hill to get a master's degree at age 55. I'm getting my master's in journalism so I can have the credentials to join a faculty as a full-time journalism instructor.

My mother taught high school and college for 44 years and went to UNC-CH to get her PhD at age 56.

Her case was different. After receiving her undergraduate degree in 1954 at UNC-Greensboro, then known as Woman's College, she earned her master's in communication during several summer school sessions at Northwestern University.

More than three decades later, in the second half of a teaching career at North Carolina State University, my mother went after her PhD both to increase her salary and to prove she could do it.

I was in high school when she started her coursework at UNC. By the time I was a freshman on the same campus, she only had a few classes left. As an immature and self-absorbed 18-year-old, I didn't think what she was doing was brave or hard or even out of the ordinary. She'd almost always taught college, so it didn't seem that different for her to go to college. Plus, she was still living in Raleigh with my dad and commuting 25 minutes to Chapel Hill a few days a week. It seemed more like college-light.

Our paths rarely crossed. I left little notes in her assigned drawer where she kept work for her portfolio in Peabody Hall. We met every couple of weeks for lunch at the Carolina Inn's cafeteria, which has since been converted into banquet space. I unexpectedly saw her once during "drop-add," which was the antiquated and complicated process students went through to change their assigned schedules. What happens now *online* in minutes then meant hours waiting *in line* at tables around the perimeter of Carmichael Gym. Best I remember, each table was for a different school within the university, and there were a lot of index cards requiring signatures involved.

I walked in and saw my mother ask one of the cutest guys on campus to borrow a pen. She was wearing her Talbots blue linen wrap skirt with flowers embroidered on the belt and her New Balance tennis shoes. If he knew she was my mother, or I had any relation to this old lady in a skirt and tennis shoes, I would be mortified. I left Carmichael and just accepted the classes I was dealt. Thus the C in Geology 200.

It's a tale as old as motherhood that children don't see their mothers, or their fathers, as real people with a life outside of parenthood. My sister and I were always flummoxed when we met Mother's former students and they said she was their favorite teacher at Needham Broughton High School or NCSU.

Our mother started teaching public speaking and English at Broughton High School when she was 28, so she was just 10 or 12 years older than many of her students. I've encountered a handful of them over the years who described sitting in her sixth-period English class on November 22, 1963. They first heard that President Kennedy was shot in Dallas over the loudspeaker piped into each classroom through a wooden box above the chalkboard shortly after 12:30 p.m. Within an hour the principal, Joseph Holiday, namesake for the current gym, sadly announced the president was dead.

My mother started crying along with many of the students, male and female. She walked over to the bookshelf, pulled out a book of poetry by English poet A.E. Housman and read "To an Athlete Dying Young."

The time you won your town the race
We chaired you through the market-place;
Man and boy stood cheering by,
And home we brought you shoulder-high.

Today, the road all runners come,
Shoulder-high we bring you home,
And set you at your threshold down,
Townsman of a stiller town.

Smart lad, to slip betimes away
From fields where glory does not stay,
And early though the laurel grows
It withers quicker than the rose.

Eyes the shady night has shut
Cannot see the record cut,
And silence sounds no worse than cheers
After earth has stopped the ears.

Now you will not swell the rout
Of lads that wore their honours out,
Runners whom renown outran
And the name died before the man.

So set, before its echoes fade,
The fleet foot on the sill of shade,
And hold to the low lintel up
The still-defended challenge-cup.

And round that early-laurelled head
Will flock to gaze the strengthless dead,
And find unwithered on its curls
The garland briefer than a girl's.

NCSU students have also shared memories of having my mom as their teacher. Some recount being in an oral interpretation course she created. My mother taught her students how to read children's books with Broadway-esque expression and audience interaction. Then she drove them to elementary schools across Raleigh and eastern North Carolina to read aloud to children. Almost half a century before US presidents, first ladies and celebrities were reading publicly to children and touting the benefits of parents doing the same, my mom and elementary school librarians, principals and teachers knew the benefits. So when college students, including a few football and basketball players, made reading cool, children who had never picked up a book started checking them out as fast as they could.

Though I'd known for most of my life that my mother was a wonderful teacher, it never crossed my mind to try her profession. Operating a crane or splitting atoms in a lab were more likely career changes for me until Susan King, the former dean of UNC Hussman School of Journalism and Media, suggested I become an adjunct professor at my alma mater.

About four months after my father died, I attended the school's NC Media and Journalism Hall of Fame celebration. I'd gone to it the first time in 1993 when my father was inducted and returned several times over the next three decades with my parents. On this night in 2022, I was on my own and caught up with King, the dean from

2012 to 2021. I first met her when my father and my cousin, Charlie Price, a pioneer in the state's public relations industry, toured the journalism school in a trip orchestrated by my second cousin Charla.

Charla created the trip to be a Christmas present for both of our beloved fathers a decade ago.

"Let's take them back to UNC, tour the new journalism building and just love on them for the day," Charla said when she proposed the excursion.

The best part of the day was being with family. A close second was meeting Susan King. Her résumé began with Walter Cronkite, took her to ABC, to Washington where she worked for NPR and as a White House correspondent, to the Carnegie Corporation, and finally to the deanship of one of the country's best journalism schools. For all her accomplishments she was relaxed and warm, accessible and genuine.

When I saw her at the 2022 Hall of Fame celebration, she asked where I was living now.

"It depends on the day. Various Airbnbs in Chapel Hill, in my sister's old room in the basement in Raleigh, in my house in St. Petersburg. At least once a week I have to go out to my car to find clean underwear in a suitcase I left in the trunk," I said. "I'm going back to St. Petersburg this summer while my son is home from school."

"I hear you. We do what we have to do," Susan said. She has had many chapters in her own life and calls herself the "queen of pivot."

"You should come back to Chapel Hill in the fall and teach," Susan said.

"I don't have my PhD or a master's. I'm not sure my undergraduate degree from UNC is still valid because I got in back in the dark ages with a high school GPA below a 4.0."

"You've worked what, 20 or 25 years, at one of the best papers in the country? You've been a reporter, a columnist, and a magazine editor? Adjuncts don't need a graduate degree," she countered.

"I've never taught one class or one hour in my life."

"You'd be great. I know it," she said.

Susan King is one of those rare people who believes her students, colleagues, friends and casual acquaintances are as accomplished and fearless as she is. She fuels them with her enthusiasm and somewhat-blind faith.

Well, I drank her overly generous Kool-Aid, and four months later I was walking into Carroll Hall to teach an introductory class on reporting and writing. I took the same class about 35 years earlier under Jim Shumaker, the no-nonsense, intimidating but sly and humorous inspiration for the comic strip *Shu*. I struggled, but the class also prompted me to change my major from advertising to news reporting,

A couple days before teaching my class, I had practiced my first-day lecture three times as I drove from Florida to North Carolina with my bloody, blender-beaten foot propped on the dashboard. I timed it three times to make sure it was one hour, thinking I'd let the students go 15 minutes early on the first day.

Perhaps I should not have allotted 10 minutes for calling the roll or another 15 for each of the 20 students to share their major and hometown. And 15 minutes was definitely too much time for them to ask me questions. So 17 minutes into the 75-minute class I had nothing left to say. Thank the journalism gods above I had grabbed a stack of *The Daily Tar Heel* newspapers on my way to class.

I passed them out and went through the paper explaining what makes for a breaking news story, a hard news story that's not breaking, a feature, an editorial, an op-ed and a column.

Noticing some students trying to use their fingers to scroll to the next page, I started from the beginning and explained that a newspaper required no electric power, however you did have to physically turn the pages.

After that little tutorial, we still had 15 minutes to make the class last at least 45 minutes. I pointed to a feature about a pop-up museum of sorts in the Coker Arboretum. Someone was mysteriously collecting objects lost in the campus garden of oaks, dogwoods, jonquils, liriope, tulips and twisted vines. The collection of objects found in the arboretum included pacifiers and Barbie shoes, an Ed Sheeran CD, sunglasses, COVID masks and keychains.

The story quoted a student saying the collection was akin to "a shrine because, like, none of it makes any sense."

I pointed out his use of "like" to milk seven more minutes out of the class.

"For a long time, reporters cleaned up the language of the people they were quoting if they used grammar or phrases different from how most people speak," I said. "But now there is more inclination to quote people in their exact words because everyone speaks in different ways and we aren't all expected to use the so-called Queen's English. If one of you was quoted saying 'like,' would you think it was a slight dig at how your generation speaks?"

"I would want them not to use it because if I sent it to my parents they'd be excited I was quoted but then bummed I said 'like,'" one student said. Several others agreed.

"I wouldn't have a problem with it at all. I wouldn't want

my language cleaned up. Because, like, that's how we talk," a student named Lexi said with a laugh. She made a great point and stretched the class to a respectable 45 minutes.

The next class I peppered in more of my experiences on the job as well as those of my colleagues. I shared news stories with famous and unknown bylines. I highlighted their own good work as well as mistakes they'd made in the daily assignment. We went four minutes over, and I never ran short of material again.

Lexi asked me to meet her at a Franklin Street coffee shop to go over some errors in her first two stories. A week later she asked me to meet her again even though her writing was improving.

We talked about the latest political news, our hometowns, her training in classical music and the difference between barbecue from her native Kansas City and that of my home state. After almost an hour when she had still not pulled her laptop out of her backpack, I asked if she needed help with anything from class.

"No, I don't. I just wanted to, like, talk to you. You're my favorite teacher," she said.

I remained cool while Sally Field's Oscar acceptance speech filled my mind: "I can't deny the fact that you like me. Right now, you like me."

At that moment in the Carolina Coffee Shop, I realized I love teaching because I connected with a total stranger and was helping her.

We all know the power of teaching because we've all had teachers who made an impression, went the extra mile or helped us with something that had nothing to do with academics. But I never dreamed I could be that person for someone else.

I certainly didn't have the impact on all of my students that I had on Lexi. But I saw them becoming better writers. I got to teach them things they never knew before. I made them laugh now and then. Perhaps with me, perhaps at me. It didn't matter. The students were getting to know each other better and class discussions were getting longer.

Now I'm the one who has to be paying attention, writing papers, taking tests and even attempting "data-assisted reporting" that calls for merging data fields to research statistics to prove or disprove a hunch.

"Mom, you can't even put your Christmas card list into Excel," Wade said when I mentioned that course. "You should take a summer school class at St. Pete College to get ready." (I also struggle to attach a photo to an email.)

Maybe my mother was just as unprepared for a few of her PhD classes. I'm lucky to have her as well as many other "queens of pivot" who took risks and made changes throughout their lives. A few kings too.

I wish some things never had to change. I wish I still read to my kids every night and they hung on every word. I wish my sister and I could still clandestinely roll our eyes at each other across our parfait glasses of cubed cherry Jell-O when somebody stopped at our table at Belk's cafeteria to discuss our father's latest editorial or tell my mom she was their favorite teacher. I wish my father still patted my knee and asked: "What does Katherine Victoria have to say for herself today?"

But life marches on. And I'm so very fortunate I've lived long enough to wear some of my honors out. Still, I get to march on with life, even if I'm a little out of sync sometimes.

Acknowledgments

First of all, I thank my later-in-life friends, some I knew well in high school or college and reconnected with when I came back to North Carolina. Some I loosely knew before and some I met for the first time during this latest chapter. As I gained new footing in Chapel Hill, Raleigh and Pine Knoll Shores, all of your new or renewed friendships have been vital to coming home again.

And, of course, I thank the longtime friends, cousins and Aunt Susan, who have been there all along. I thank my St. Petersburg village for continuing to be crucial and constant in my life whether I'm three states away or back in the 'burg.

Thank you, Olivia, Charlotte and Wade who had to routinely ask: "Can I stay in my room or is there a renter in our house?" when you were back home. Still, you didn't complain about your mother's nomadic lifestyle and even said you were proud of this unexpected and inconvenient phase of my life. Though I have felt untethered at times, and you don't need me or see me as often as you used to, which is as it should be, you three are my foremost purpose and biggest pride. Always.

I thank my wonderful mother who has set an example of strength, faith and love my whole life. Your independence and chin-up ways since your beloved of 64 years died, have inspired me even more.

I thank Nora for being not just a really talented editor but also a calming, patient, astute and encouraging friend.

Thank you, Kelly, who designed and copyedited this book, and was even more careful with my words than I was. (A Wisconsin girl and a Raleigh girl walked into a Carrboro coffee shop and found they were almost the same person.)

Alli, I love how your pen and mind work to make yet another book much better.

Hannah, my publicist, you got me from our first phone call. You found an audience for this book and reassured me all along the way.

Thank you, Zack, for securing the most authentic fake blood the World Wide Web has to offer, and for giving this cover all of your New York Times expertise.

Biz, thank you for styling me, providing the backdrop and suggesting we place the Ninja blade sideways. And for always being there when I'm a little sideways.

I thank my UNC MEJO 153 students who unknowingly prompted me to try for a career in teaching. Connecting with you, helping you become better writers and reporters, making you laugh, reading your reviews and your warm greetings on campus led me to a completely unexpected path in life. Remember, there are so many paths.

I especially thank the readers of this book. Anytime I hear someone I know—or a total stranger— say that something I wrote made you laugh, or cry, or think of something in your own life, I am appreciative and surprised.

My father often told me that connecting with readers was the second-best gift in his life after his family. I have nowhere near his reach or ability, but I have come to understand how right he was.

And, thank you Daddy.

She Writes Press, 2020

First Place Winner, Uplifting & Inspiring Nonfiction,
2020 Chanticleer International Book Awards

One of top 10 nonfiction best sellers for 2020 at Tombolo Books
in St. Petersburg, Florida

Tampa Bay Times Best Books of 2020 list

Praise from *Southern Literary Review*:

Smith's collection of personal essays offers glimpses into the
life of a journalist who is also a daughter, sister, wife, mother,
friend, employer, woman, human being.... Smith knows her craft
well. She is a sharp observer, skilled writer and an engaging and
entertaining storyteller.... The varied textures and richness of

the experiences and Smith's openness and vulnerability endear the narrator to readers. We don't want this new friendship to end and can only hope that Smith continues writing, sharing new chapters of her life, offering us frequent laughs, but always touching our emotions and opening our eyes to new sights and insights.

Praise from Tracy Babiasz in *Booklist*,
American Library Association:

Southern women frequently are taught to follow the rules, from proper party etiquette to why sending fan mail is tacky. Smith, a journalist-turned-public relations specialist, regularly finds herself breaking one rule or another and recounts her experiences in this delightful essay collection. She is under no illusion about the mistakes she's made.... Smith writes of going her own way with humor and honesty, encouraging readers not to take themselves too seriously and find value in friends and family. Readers of essays from Sloane Crosley, Samantha Irby or Bailey White will laugh out loud.

— *About the Author* —

Raleigh native Katherine Snow Smith has lived throughout the south as a newspaper reporter, editor, daughter, sister, mother, wife, divorcee, adjunct instructor and friend. She's worked at small town papers and business journals, but spent most of her career at the esteemed *Tampa Bay Times*. A few decades (no need to count them) after graduating from UNC-Chapel Hill with a degree in journalism, she's getting her master's at her alma mater so she can teach on a college level. Katherine, who has three 20-something children, divides her time between Chapel Hill, North Carolina, and St. Petersburg, Florida.